8

Progressive Multiple Choice English

Compiled by
A. F. BOLT
Head of Department of English
and General Studies at
Esher County Grammar School

HARRAP LONDON

NOTE

**A list of answers to questions
is obtainable from the publishers,
and will be sent free to
teachers on receipt of a large
stamped addressed envelope**

By the same author:

Multiple Choice English

First published in Great Britain 1974
by George G. Harrap & Co. Ltd
182–184 High Holborn, London WC1V 7AX

ISBN 0 245 52022 8

*Composed in 11 on 12 pt. Linotype Times type and
printed by Western Printing Services Ltd, Bristol
Made in Great Britain*

Introduction

In this book of multiple choice comprehension exercises the passages are, I hope, long enough to be interesting reading matter in their own right, and useful as stimuli to further reading and writing. The use of the multiple choice technique as a teaching process can, I believe, be a useful ally to the traditional open-ended question, discussion and answer method. When a multiple choice exercise is used in a learning situation, a careful appraisal of the alternative answers is essential, and a justification of the final choice will make the student go through those procedures of reference and reasoning which are so important in comprehending other people's words. I believe this to be a very important part of the use of these exercises, and the exchange of ideas and viewpoints when students come to different conclusions provides a useful group situation. For this reason the key has been kept separate from the exercises and should only be used when discussion has ended.

Some teachers are bothered by the idea that one answer only should be considered as correct: they feel that degrees of 'correctness' should be recognized and that some acknowledgment should be given to the 'near correct' answer. In the teaching situation discussion will make the 'degree of correctness' clear, but it is hoped that it will also make it clear why one answer only is the *best* possible. In examination, it is by grading the degrees of difficulty of each item in a whole battery of questions (50 or 60 at least) that a process of real selection can be achieved. The handful of items with a difficult choice of correct answers will be those that search out the highest level of perception in the student.

As an examination technique multiple choice methods are well established and are used by many examining boards. The student, however, will benefit from some practice in answering questions in this form, if only because he will then face a situation in which a familiar technique is being used and he will be confident in his approach. I must add the same warning that I gave in *Multiple Choice English* that naturally, I do not claim that the exercises in

3

this book have been submitted to the rigorous pre-testing procedure that examination papers demand. Nevertheless, they have been worked over and most carefully checked.

For these reasons I submit these exercises to the reader, and I hope that they will be found interesting, stimulating and useful.

Author's Note

In compiling this book I have received help in a number of ways from a number of people and I would like to express my appreciation to: the often unwitting cooperation of students, the advice from friends and colleagues, the long-suffering patience of my family, the eagle-eyed vigilance from Mrs Sweet, my typist, and, finally, the encouragement of Christine Adams who sped this book to completion by making the work a pleasure.

A.F.B.

1

He was at the hall early on the night of the play and made up and dressed in the police constable's uniform by the end of the first act. As the second act began he found himself alone in the dressing-room. He looked into the mirror and squared the helmet on his head. He certainly looked the part all right. It would be a bit of a lark to go out in the street and pinch somebody for speeding or something. He narrowed his eyes, looking fiercely at himself, and spoke his opening line in a gutteral undertone.

Well, this was it. No good looking in the book. If he didn't know the part now he never would. Out there the second act was under way, the players doing their very best, revelling in a hobby they loved, giving entertainment to all those people and in return the audience was thrilling to every twist and climax of the plot, and not letting one witty phrase, one humorous exchange go by without a laugh. A good audience, Mrs Bostock had said: the sort of audience all actors, professional or amateur, loved: at one with the players, receptive, responsive, appreciative. And soon its eyes would be on him.

He was suddenly seized by an appalling attack of stage fright. His stomach was empty, a hollow void of fear. He put his head in his hands. He couldn't do it. How could he ever have imagined he could? He couldn't face all those people. His mouth was dry and when he tried to bring his lines to memory he found nothing but a blank.

A knock on the door made him look up. He felt panic grip him now. Had he missed his entrance? Had he ruined the performance for everybody by cringing here like a frightened child? The knock was repeated and Mrs Bostock's voice said from outside, 'Are you there, Mr Royston?'

Albert took his script in his hands and opened the door. She smiled brightly up at him. 'Everything all right?' She gave him an appraising look. 'You look wonderful. You're not on for a little while yet but I should come and stand in the wings and get the feel of the action. You look a bit pale about the gills. What's wrong—stage fright?'

'It's all a bit new to me,' Albert said feebly.

'Of course it is. But you know your lines perfectly and once you're out there you'll forget your nervousness. Just remember the audience is on your side.'

They went up the narrow steps to the level of the stage. The 40 voices of the actors became more distinct. He caught the tail-end of a line he recognized. There already? Recurrent fear gripped his stomach.

He looked out on to the brightly lit stage, at the actors moving about, talking, and across to where the girl who was acting as prompter sat with an open script on her knee. 'Shirley hasn't had a thing to do so far,' Mrs Bostock murmured. 'The whole thing's gone like a dream.' She took the script from Albert's hands and found the place for him. 'Here we are. Now you just follow the action in there and relax; take it easy. You'll be on and off so 50 quick you'll hardly know you've left the wings.'

'I'm all right now,' Albert told her.

He realized to his own surprise that he was; and he became increasingly so as the action of the play absorbed him, so that he began to feel himself part of it and no longer a frightened amateur shivering in the wings.

Two pages to go. The younger son was telling his brother about the accident. The row was just beginning and at the very height of it he would make his entrance. He began to feel excited. What was it Mrs Bostock had said? 'From the second you step on you dom- 60 inate the stage. Your entrance is like a thunder-clap.' By shots! He realized vaguely that Mrs Bostock had left his side, but he didn't care now. He felt a supreme confidence. He was ready. He'd show them. By shots he would!

One page. '"You've been rotten all your life, Paul"' the elder brother was saying. '"I've never cherished any illusion about you, but this, this is more than ever I dreamed you were capable of."'

'"I know you hate me, Tom. I've always known it. But if only for father's sake, you must help me now. You know what it will do to him if he finds out. He couldn't stand it in his condition."' 70

'"You swine. You utter swine...."'

The girl who was the maid appeared at his side. She gave him a quick smile. No nerves about her. She'd been on and off the stage all evening, living the part. Albert stared out, fascinated. Not

6

until this moment had he known the true thrill of acting, of sub-merging one's own personality in that of another.

"'Where are you going?'"

"'I'm going to find that man you knocked down and get him to hospital. And you're coming with me.'"

"'But it's too late, Tom. It was hours ago. Someone's sure to have found him by now. Perhaps the police. . . .'" 80

Any minute now. They were working up to his entrance. *Like a thunder-clap.* Albert braced his shoulders and touched his helmet. He glanced down at the script and quickly turned a page. He had lost his place. Panic smote him like a blow. They were still talking, though, so he must be all right. And anyway the maid gave him his cue and she was still by his side. Then suddenly she was no longer at his side. She had gone. He fumbled with his script. Surely . . . not so far. . . .

He felt Mrs Bostock at his elbow. He turned to her in stupid 90 surprise.

'But,' he said, 'they've . . . they've—'

She nodded. 'Yes. They've skipped three pages. They've missed your part right out.'

He was already at home when Alice returned.

'Whatever happened, Albert?' she said anxiously. 'You weren't ill, were you?'

He told her. 'I went and got changed straight away,' he said, 100 'and came home.'

'Well, isn't that a shame!'

'Oh, they just got carried away,' Albert said. 'One of 'em lost his place and skipped and the other had to follow him. They did it so quickly nobody could do owt about it.' He smiled as he began to take off his shoes. 'Looks as though I'll never know whether I'd've stood up to it or not,' he said.

He never did anything of the kind again.

A long time after he was able to face with equanimity his wife's request, in the presence of acquaintances, that he should tell them 110 about his 'acting career', and say, 'No, you tell 'em, Alice. You tell it best.' And the genuine smile on his honest face during the recounting of the story of the unspoken lines, which never failed to provoke shouts of laughter, always deceived the listeners. So that never for one moment did they guess just how cruel, how grievous a disappointment it had been to him at the time.

7

1. For which one of the following reasons can it most reasonably be assumed that Albert was not really a policeman?
   A. He was acting the part of a policeman in a play.
   B. He thought it would be a lark to arrest someone.
   C. He was embarrassed by his experience.
   D. He seems to be lacking self-confidence.
   E. He was suffering from stage fright.

2. The last sentence of the first paragraph implies that
   A. he was angry with himself
   B. he was a foreigner
   C. he was not an educated man
   D. he was rehearsing his part
   E. he did not want to take part

3. The sentence 'Well, this was it' (line 9) implies that
   A. this was an unpleasant experience
   B. this was a pleasant experience
   C. he had been waiting for this moment
   D. he had been expecting trouble
   E. things were about to go wrong

4. The word 'revelling' (line 11) could best be replaced by
   A. engaging
   B. entertaining
   C. acting
   D. delighting
   E. succeeding

5. A good audience, according to Mrs Bostock, is all of the following *except*
   A. responsive
   B. humorous
   C. receptive
   D. appreciative
   E. sympathetic

6. Some of the following are mentioned as indications of stage fright:
   (i) His mouth was dry.
   (ii) He had forgotten his lines.
   (iii) He felt faint.
   (iv) He spoke feebly.
   (v) He behaved childishly.

Are they
A. (i), (ii), (iii)?
B. (ii), (iii), (iv)?
C. (iii), (iv), (v)?
D. (i), (ii), (iv)?
E. (i), (iii), (iv)?

7. Mrs Bostock gave him an 'appraising look' (line 32) because
   A. she was critical of his make-up
   B. she admired his acting
   C. she wanted to encourage him
   D. she was estimating how nervous he was
   E. she approved of his appearance

8. The word 'feebly' (line 36) is used to imply that
   A. Albert was nervous
   B. Albert's reply was rather obvious
   C. Albert was unwell
   D. Albert was not very bright
   E. Albert did not want his voice to carry

9. The sentence 'He caught the tail-end of a line he recognized' means
   A. the way to the stage was familiar
   B. he began to remember his part
   C. he needed help to climb the stairs
   D. he heard familiar lines from the play
   E. he tried to relax by thinking of familiar things

10. The word 'recurrent' (line 42) means that the fear
    A. keeps returning
    B. makes him want to run away
    C. is only temporary
    D. is menacing and painful
    E. affects his whole body

11. When Mrs Bostock says 'The whole thing's gone like a dream',
    she implies that
    A. everything is too good to last
    B. the play is not dealing with reality
    C. their success is only an illusion
    D. nothing has gone wrong
    E. what has happened was unpredictable

12. When Mrs Bostock speaks of 'wings' (line 51) she refers to
    A. the dressing-room area
    B. part of the stage
    C. the speed of the action
    D. the nervousness of Albert
    E. the inspiration of the actors

13. The words 'Your entrance is like a thunder-clap' imply that when Albert goes on the stage
    A. he will have everyone's attention
    B. he will make the audience afraid
    C. the actors will appear afraid
    D. he will speak in a loud voice
    E. the audience will applaud loudly

14. What Mrs Bostock says and does between line 46 and line 47 is most likely to
    A. encourage Albert
    B. irritate Albert
    C. make Albert nervous
    D. embarrass Albert
    E. make Albert laugh

15. From the information in the passage there must be at least how many characters in the play?
    A. Two.
    B. Three.
    C. Four.
    D. Five.
    E. We cannot tell.

16. The words 'I've never cherished any illusion about you' suggest that the speaker was
    A. realistic
    B. unsympathetic
    C. impolite
    D. disappointed
    E. disillusioned

17. Albert finds that the 'thrill of acting' is
    A. in the excitement of performing
    B. waiting for one's entrance on stage
    C. meeting people with similar interests

10

D. losing oneself in the character one plays

E. the friendliness and encouragement of other actors

18. The words '*Like a thunder-clap*' (line 83) are in italics because
    A. they are the climax of the passage
    B. they are not a complete sentence
    C. they are quoted from elsewhere in the passage
    D. they are used in a figurative sense
    E. they need to stand out and be emphatic

19. The sentence 'Panic smote him like a blow' is an example of some of the following literary devices:
    (i) Exaggeration.
    (ii) Comparison
    (iii) Personification.
    (iv) Emphasis.
    Is it
    A. (i) and (ii)?
    B. (ii) and (iii)?
    C. (iii) and (iv)?
    D. (i) and (iii)?
    E. (ii) and (iv)?

20. Albert lost his place (line 85) because
    A. he was nervous
    B. he turned the page too quickly
    C. the maid went before he expected it
    D. the actors omitted some of the words
    E. he fumbled with the script

21. It can be assumed from the passage that Alice spoke anxiously (line 98) because
    A. he was already at home
    B. he looked unwell
    C. he had not appeared on stage
    D. he had returned home without her
    E. he had changed his clothes

22. When Albert says 'they just got carried away' he is referring to
    A. the rest of the actors in the play
    B. the actors playing the part of the brothers
    C. the reaction of the audience

11

D. the producer who became angry

E. the maid and the prompter

23. The word 'equanimity' (line109) could best be replaced by
    A. resignation
    B. amusement
    C. annoyance
    D. calmness
    E. impartiality

24. By describing Albert's smile as 'genuine' and his face as 'honest' the author
    A. refers sarcastically to Albert's character
    B. indicates how disappointed Albert was
    C. shows how amused Albert had become
    D. shows how Albert's visitors were deceived
    E. underlines how true the wife's account is

25. The dramatic effect of the last sentence in the passage is gained
    A. by careful attention to word order
    B. by the use of a wide-ranging vocabulary
    C. because the final sentence is always dramatic
    D. because it becomes sentimental in tone.
    E. by summarizing the content of the whole passage

2

Saunders had half fallen asleep; a voice at his side woke him.'The fog's getting thick, sir.'

It was already dense, with the first light touching it with dusty yellow, and he would have sworn at the policeman for not waking him earlier if his stammer had not made him chary of wasting words. He said: 'Pass the word round to move in.'

'Are we going to rush the place, sir?'

'No. There's the girl there. We can't have any s-s-shooting. Wait till he comes out.'

But the policeman hadn't left his side when he noticed, 'The door's opening.' Saunders put his whistle in his mouth and lowered his safety catch. The light was bad and the fog deceptive; but he recognized the dark coat as it slipped to the right into the shelter of the coal trucks. He blew his whistle and was after it. The black coat had half a minute's start and was moving quickly into the fog. It was impossible to see at all more than twenty feet ahead. But Saunders kept doggedly just in sight blowing his whistle contin-uously. As he hoped, the whistle blew in front; it confused the fugitive; he hesitated for a moment and Saunders gained on him. They had him cornered, and this Saunders knew was the dan-gerous moment. He blew his whistle urgently three times into the fog to bring the police round in a complete circle and the whistle was taken up in the yellow obscurity, passing in a wide invisible circle.

But he had lost pace, the fugitive spurted forward and was lost. Saunders blew two blasts: 'Advance slowly and keep in touch.' To the right and in front a single long whistle announced that the man had been seen, and the police converged on the sound. Each kept in touch with a policeman on either hand. It was impossible as long as the circle was kept closed for the man to escape. But the circle drew in and there was no sign of him; the short single

13

exploratory blasts sounded petulant and lost. At last Saunders gazing ahead saw the faint form of a policeman come out of the fog a dozen yards away. He halted them all with a whistled signal: the fugitive must be somewhere just ahead in the tangle of trucks in the centre. Revolver in hand Saunders advanced and a policeman took his place and closed the circle.

Suddenly Saunders spied his man. He had taken up a strategic position where a pile of coal and an empty truck at his back made a wedge which guarded him from surprise. He was invisible to the 40 police behind him, and he had turned sideways like a duellist and presented only a shoulder to Saunders, while a pile of old sleepers hid him to the knees. It seemed to Saunders that it meant only one thing, that he was going to shoot it out; the man must be mad and desperate. The hat was pulled down over the face; the coat hung in an odd loose way; the hands were in the pockets. Saunders called at him through the yellow coils of fog: 'You'd better come quietly.' He raised his pistol and advanced, his fingers ready on the trigger. But the immobility of the figure scared him. It was in shadow half hidden in the swirl of fog. It was he who was exposed, 50 with the east, and the pale penetration of early light, behind him. It was like waiting for execution, for he could not fire first. But all the same, knowing what Mather felt, knowing that this man was mixed up with Mather's girl, he did not want much excuse to fire. Mather would stand by him. A movement would be enough. He said sharply without a stammer: 'Put up your hands!' The figure didn't move. He told himself again with a kindling hatred for the man who had injured Mather: I'll plug him if he doesn't obey: they'll all stand by me: one more chance. 'Put up your hands!' and when the figure stayed as it was with its hands hidden, a hardly 60 discernible menace, he fired.

But as he pressed the trigger a whistle blew, a long urgent blast which panted and gave out like a rubber animal, from the direction of the wall and the road. There could be no doubt whatever what that meant, and suddenly he saw it all: he had shot at Mather's girl; she'd drawn them off. He screamed at the men behind him: 'Back to the gate!' and ran forward. He had seen her waver at his shot. He said: 'Are you hurt?' and knocked the hat off her head to see her better.

'You're the third person who's tried to kill me,' Anne said 70 weakly, leaning hard against the truck. 'Come to sunny Nottwich. Well, I've got six lives left.'

Saunder's stammer came back: 'W-w-w-w.'

'This is where you hit,' Anne said, 'if that's what you want to

14

'know,' showing the long yellow sliver on the edge of the truck. 'It was only an outer. You don't even get a box of chocolates.'

1. The events take place
   A. in early evening
   B. at night
   C. in early morning
   D. in late afternoon
   E. at mid-day

2. The word 'chary' (line 5) could best be replaced by
   A. careful
   B. cautious
   C. impatient
   D. cheerful
   E. conscious

3. In the sentence beginning 'The light was bad ...' (line 12) it is implied that
   A. the fog hid everything from view
   B. the fog was not of equal density everywhere
   C. it was not as foggy as it seemed
   D. it was difficult to use the lights in the fog
   E. one could not be sure of recognizing things in the fog

4. The use of the word 'slipped' (line 13) suggests that the movement was
   A. careless
   B. dangerous
   C. awkward
   D. furtive
   E. agile

5. The fugitive was confused (line18) because
   A. he could not see where he was going
   B. he did not recognize the place
   C. he was being followed
   D. he did not expect to hear the whistle ahead
   E. the whistle behind was gaining on him

6. The phrase 'passing in a wide invisible circle' (line 23) refers to some of the following:
   (i) A succession of blasts on whistles.
   (ii) A number of whistles blowing at the same time.
   (iii) Men hidden by the fog.
   (iv) Police hiding from the fugitive.
   (v) The arrangement of the houses.
   Is it
   A. (i) and (iv) only?
   B. (ii) and (iii) only?
   C. (i) and (iii) only?
   D. (iv) and (v) only?
   E. (i) and (v) only?

7. Which of the following signals is *not* mentioned as part of the code of whistling used by the police?
   A. Three blasts.
   B. Repeated blasts.
   C. Two blasts.
   D. Alternate long and short blasts.
   E. Short sharp blasts.

8. The use of the word 'petulant' (line 32) suggests
   A. the police were worried
   B. the sound was faint
   C. a feeling of disappointment
   D. the police were getting tired
   E. a feeling of urgency

9. The position was 'strategic' (line 38) because
   A. it was advantageous to the man
   B. the man was uncomfortable
   C. the situation was desperate
   D. it was dangerous for the man
   E. the man had to stand up

10. Saunders thought the man would 'shoot it out' (line 43) because
   A. he was mad
   B. he was desperate
   C. he was hiding
   D. he was turned sideways on
   E. he was armed

16

11. The coat hung in an 'odd loose way' (line 45) because
   A. the man was hiding
   B. the man was turned sideways
   C. it was too large
   D. it was old and worn
   E. it covered his weapons

12. When Saunders advanced (line 48) he was scared because
   A. he thought the man was armed
   B. the man was hidden by the sleepers
   C. he could not see the man clearly
   D. the man did not move
   E. the man was turned sideways

13. Saunders felt exposed because
   A. he was out in the open
   B. he was silhouetted in the early light
   C. he felt cold in the morning air
   D. the light was shining on him
   E. he could not fire first

14. Which of the following statements reflects Saunders' attitude?
   A. He did not wish to fire until Mather was present.
   B. He expected Mather would support him if he fired.
   C. He did not wish to be an executioner.
   D. He needed a good excuse to fire.
   E. He thought Mather's girl did not understand what was happening.

15. 'A movement would be enough' (line 54)
   A. to provide an excuse to fire
   B. to identify the man
   C. to give the man a target
   D. to show Mather's support for Saunders
   E. because words were unnecessary

16. The implication of the use of the word 'kindling' (line 56) is that his hatred was
   A. sympathetic
   B. intense
   C. weakened by fear
   D. of short duration
   E. growing in intensity

17

17. The description of the whistle blast which 'panted and gave out like a rubber animal' (line 62) is so described because
    A. the note was shrill and squeaky
    B. the noise faded out slowly
    C. the note sounded urgent
    D. the policeman had been running
    E. the policeman was surprised by the shot

18. The clause 'she'd drawn them off' (line 66) means that she had
    A. wanted Saunders to shoot
    B. now removed her coat and hat
    C. carefully planned her movements
    D. underestimated the skill of the police
    E. deliberately led them in the wrong direction

19. The word 'waver' (line 68) could best be replaced by
    A. move
    B. stagger
    C. recoil
    D. sway
    E. gesture

20. Anne's first words (line 69) suggest that she
    A. was frightened
    B. was delirious
    C. had a sense of humour
    D. had no respect for the police
    E. was angry

3

The General hoped, as he came out on to the sunlit rooftop terrace of his house, that the concert would be a success. He stood with hands in pockets, looking away from the sound of gunfire, his eye catching the slow brown snake of a convoy coiling along a road towards a distant village. The sky had cleared except for grey cloud smudges on the fortified hills, and he wished the rain wouldn't return for some days so that extra reserves of ammunition could be carried to the front. Turning slightly, he saw that the main street of the village was now cleared of rubble, edged by shells of houses and the deposited slag-heaps of bricks and mortar. Farm-buildings dotted beyond, having escaped the loop of destruction he had thrown around them, gave shelter to lightly-wounded resting after the battle. In another part of the village gangs of impressed civilians were repairing houses for the winter, scurrying over them willingly enough, carrying straw baskets of cement and tiles, while in the centre-square troops were standing in line to draw rations.

He was pleasantly moved by such signs of organization unfolding in every direction. The foothill masking positions were as perfectly dug, placed, supported and camouflaged as his knowledge and intuition could make them, for during the morning he had driven from one to another inspecting the most important. A few months would see the beginning of the 'big' offensive, and his anticipation of success made him impatient almost to the point of unhappiness. He had never previously known such a feeling in his pre-attack moods, and for the first time he began to label those that were less harmful: taciturnity, drunkenness, extensive planning that sometimes went on too long and contradicted itself, bringing on insomnia—but never impatience, never that cloven-hoofed quality that had sent so many commanders into exile.

Yet on thinking of the evening's entertainment—sounds of

preparation for it came from the barn across the road—his mind was lightened by muted and more agreeable waiting that gave him access to unknown emotions. He had looked forward to symphonies as a young man—when they could still be played—but the one he would soon be hearing was divided from those by a gap measured more in events than time, and for him to explore this gap meant an immersion into milestones of slaughter and blood that had refused the minor poetic rhythms of music because they had no place in the art of war. Their absence had been felt, and he would experience their return with the depth and understanding given to him by middle-age. 40

A sudden breeze turned him from the balustrade, so that he was again aware of activity in the barn—the harsh sound of instruments being tuned, movement of furniture, discussion over some no doubt insignificant crisis—and he closed his eyes as if to increase the comfort this noise gave him. The sound of war's preparation drifted away from his senses, and suddenly, on opening his eyes to the green plain and white houses beyond the village, he was faced with clear and cruel perspective by the fact that the 50 orchestra which was to perform for him that night would have to be destroyed in two days time.

He could not believe it, and only knew it to be true when the full history of High Command's order came back to him. He shielded his eyes, as if the sun were too strong for them, or as if to hide from his mind a ghastly vision of planned execution. These thoughts promised to destroy his enjoyment of the concert, and in a more reasonable mood he told himself that the orchestra would have been already dead had he followed the High Command's order on first receiving the signal. I'm doing all I can, he justified 60 himself from an abyss of weariness. A short, calm, isolated man, he stood by the parapet looking away from the house but taking in little now of the landscape detail: only an impressionistic confusion of colours worked their way into his cogitations. His mind went over the same facts like a too repetitive alliteration: the accidental capture of the orchestra, the decision submitted to High Command, the signal saying they were to be shot, and his capitulation to a slowly mounting desire to hear a symphony. Now he would hear one, the orchestra would be destroyed, and his life would go on as before. 70

1. The metaphorical use of the word 'snake' (line 4) is most appropriate for which of the following reasons?
   A. The convoy is moving slowly.
   B. The convoy is stretched out along the winding road.
   C. The convoy appears brown on the road.
   D. The convoy is moving away from trouble.
   E. The convoy represents a danger to the enemy.

2. The 'smudges' on the hill (line 6) refer to
   A. fortifications
   B. the moving convoys
   C. the pattern of the fields
   D. drifting clouds
   E. flooded areas

3. The village had been captured after it had been
   A. surrounded
   B. bombed
   C. flooded
   D. burnt
   E. evacuated

4. The word 'willingly' (line 15) is used as a contrast to which of the following words used in the passage?
   A. Scurrying.
   B. Wounded.
   C. Gangs.
   D. Troops.
   E. Impressed.

5. The villagers worked willingly because
   A. they liked the soldiers
   B. they wished to care for the wounded
   C. the work was easy
   D. they were to draw their rations
   E they were repairing their houses

6. A foothill is
   A. a small hill
   B. a kind of gun
   C. a fortification
   D. a resting place
   E. a measure

21

7. The word 'intuition' (line 21) could best be replaced **by**
   A. instructions
   B. learning
   C. feelings
   D. imagination
   E. advice

8. The General's feeling of 'unhappiness' (line 25) was caused by
   A. success
   B. impatience
   C. moodiness
   D. his inspection
   E. the offensive

9. The General suffered from insomnia when
   A. he anticipated success
   B. he was drunk
   C. he was excited
   D. his campaigns were extensive
   E. his plans were too protracted

10. The word 'taciturnity' (line 27) means
   A. gloominess
   B. indecision
   C. silence
   D. lack of appetite
   E. thoughtfulness

11. It is implied that the most harmful mood is that of
   A. intuition
   B. drunkenness
   C. insomnia
   D. impatience
   E. unhappiness

12. The quality of impatience is 'cloven-hoofed' because
   A. it represents something foolish
   B. it is a sign of obstinacy
   C. it is a temptation from the devil
   D. it is a sign of sickness
   E. it is only half-human

13. The word 'muted' (line 33) has the meaning of
   A. soft
   B. musical
   C. relaxed
   D. unemotional
   E. quiet

14. In the context of the passage the words 'when they could still be played' are most likely to mean
   A. before war stopped the playing
   B. while the players still had the skill to play
   C. before political considerations affected playing
   D. while the music was still available
   E. before the players had been killed or wounded

15. The 'milestones of slaughter and blood' (line 38) are
   A. poems that the General has read
   B. the journeys that he has taken
   C. the various wars in which he has fought
   D. the violent events of his own life
   E. the wounds that he has suffered

16. The 'perspective' referred to (line 50) is
   A. the harsh sounds of the orchestra
   B. the green fields and white houses
   C. the signs of war in the surrounding country
   D. the impending fate of the orchestra
   E. the sounds of war's preparation

17. From the passage the General could be described as all the following *except*
   A. lonely
   B. sentimental
   C. musical
   D. humane
   E. rational

18. The words 'I'm doing all I can' imply a feeling of
   A. optimism
   B. self-satisfaction
   C. weariness
   D. hopelessness
   E. efficiency

19. The word 'abyss' (line 61), here used figuratively, is associated with
A. depth
B. danger
C. darkness
D. steepness
E. religion

20. The word 'cogitations' (line 64) could best be replaced by
A. memories
B. fears
C. impressions
D. thoughts
E. plans

21. The General's desire to hear a symphony
A. was a sign of loneliness
B. was the result of a sudden impulse
C. led hm to spend a good deal of money
D. was achieved after a personal struggle
E. was a splendid idea

22. The mood of the General at the end of the passage could best be described as
A. cheerful
B. confident
C. contented
D. complacent
E. calm

4

'It's Mr Lumley, isn't it?' said the man at last.

'That's my name,' Charles assented cautiously, mumbling on in a rapid undertone, 'not sure where had the pleasure remember face of course, let me see.'

The woman, who clearly did not share in the embarrassment, leaned forward with an encouraging smile.

'We're George Hutchins's mother and dad,' she volunteered kindly. 'We met you when we came up to see him at the College.'

At once Charles remembered a scene which he would gladly have forgotten. George Hutchins, an unpleasantly dogged and humourless young man, had lived on the same staircase and had indulged a taste for lecturing Charles on the virtues of hard work. 'No system,' he would say contemptuously, looking round at Charles's bookcase, 'just a random collection of texts, no real system. You're just playing at it. Now I can't afford to play at it, I go over each little plot of the subject carefully. Preliminary survey, then a closer reading, and then, three months later, revision. And the whole thing's tied up. That's how these men like Lockwood have got where they are, and I'm going after them.' Lockwood was a dreary whey-faced tutor of the college for whom Hutchins had a deep and sincere admiration, and who encouraged him along the road to complacent prigdom. After one of these lectures, Charles would sit staring into the fire, inert and crumpled; the half-fantastic, half-shrewd gleams and pin-points of intuition which served him as a substitute for intellectual method damped and fizzling out in the clammy atmosphere of Hutchins's brutal efficiency.

'I s'pose you've heard all about George's success,' said Mr Hutchins; his voice was bright and confident, but with a curious undertone of bewilderment and pathos. 'He's got a Fellowship,' he added, using the strange word in inverted commas, grafting it like some strange twig on to the stunted trunk of his artisan's vocabulary.

For the next few minutes the conversation arranged itself on purely mechanical lines; a steady flow of 'deserve congratulations worked hard for it now got it' *clichés* from Charles, and an answering dribble of 'Well it's what he's always wanted not that it hasn't been a struggle' from the withered couple opposite. Behind the mask Charles was genuinely sorry for them; it was so obvious that they were even more bewildered than on the day, two years ago, when he had walked into Hutchins's room with a request for the loan of a toasting-fork and found the three sitting dumbly and stiffly together. Hutchins had been so abjectly and obviously ashamed of his parents' working-class appearance and manner that he had tried to avoid introducing them, evidently in the hope that Charles would not realize the relationship. But the family likeness had proclaimed itself and Charles had lingered, chatting for a few minutes, partly out of a genuine desire to comfort these decent and kindly people, to show them that if their son was an ungainly snob, there were others who were not, and to try to give them a few pleasant minutes in what was so clearly a disastrous visit. They had never appeared again, and Hutchins had never mentioned them. Charles, with no other intention than to be pleasant, had once asked him if his parents were keeping well, but the scowl he had received in answer had made it clear that Hutchins had regarded the question as a simple insult. The raw cult of success by which he lived could allow of no tolerance of the couple who had spawned him; they were neither prosperous nor celebrated, their Birmingham speech exposed in an instant the unreality of his own diction (an unbelievably exact reproduction of Lockwood's donnish snivelling), and, in short, his resentment of them could go no farther. Amid all the problems that beset him, Charles found time to rejoice that he was not as Hutchins was, that his soul, stretched as it was on the rack of his ludicrous predicament, was alive. He was not given to quoting, but a favourite fragment swam into his head, and he muttered, 'I am one of those who have created, even if it be but a world of agony.' 'Beg pardon?' said Mr Hutchins, surprised, leaning forward. 'Just nothing, just nothing,' Charles replied; he wished to sound airy and nonchalant but the words rang out brassily and the effect was one of impertinence. In despair he stood up, dragged his case down from the rack, gabbled 'Must get ready getting out next station,' and fled down the corridor in search of a fresh compartment. The only one that appeared to have a vacant seat was occupied by four blue-chinned men banging down cards on a suitcase, who looked up at him with such hostility that he retreated again, and, fearing to stand in the corridor lest Mr and Mrs Hutchins should come out and see him, spent the forty minutes that remained of his journey cowering in the lavatory.

1. Charles's caution and mumbling was caused by the fact that .
   A. he did not wish to be recognized
   B. he wanted to be left alone
   C. he was embarrassed by not recognizing the man
   D. he did not like George Hutchins
   E. he wanted to forget an unpleasant scene

2. The word 'assented' (line 2) could best be replaced by
   A. agreed
   B. murmured
   C. approved
   D. muttered
   E. spoke

3. The use of the word 'indulged' (line 12) suggests that Hutchins
   A. was an easy-going young man
   B. enjoyed lecturing Lumley
   C. lectured Lumley in an unpleasant way
   D. thought it was funny to see Charles's lack of system
   E. was a hardworking and serious student

4. The sentence 'And the whole thing's tied up' (line 18) means here that Hutchins
   A. was ready to pass on his knowledge
   B. referred to the difficulty of the work
   C. has done all the work he thinks necessary
   D. was referring to Lumley's untidy methods
   E. was showing how clever he was

5. The expression 'whey-faced' (line 20) refers to
   A. the shape of the tutor's face
   B. the expression on the tutor's face
   C. the character of the tutor
   D. the size of the tutor's face
   E. the colour of the tutor's face

27

6. It is suggested that Hutchins's tutor encouraged him to become

    A. a dry and dull scholar

    B. a rude and objectionable man

    C. a selfish and snobbish man

    D. a self-satisfied and self-righteous man

    E. an easy-going but self-centred man

7. In the passage beginning 'the half-fantastic, half-shrewd. . .' (line 24) down to 'brutal efficiency' (line 26), which of the following words contains most completely the imagery of the metaphor employed?

    A. Light.

    B. Fire.

    C. Water.

    D. Flame.

    E. Heat.

8. The descriptions of Hutchins and Lockwood in the paragraph beginning 'At once Charles remembered. . .' (line 9) are the product of

    A. close and accurate observations

    B. emotive and subjective writing

    C. a keenly sarcastic style

    D. class-conscious prejudice

    E. dramatic and detailed vocabulary

9. The word 'intuition' (line 24) refers to

    A. an instinctive feeling

    B. a method of learning

    C. an attitude of self-reliance

    D. a scholarly confidence

    E. an exceptional intelligence

10. Mr Hutchins used the words 'in inverted commas' because

    A. it is printed with a capital letter

    B. it refers to a particular appointment

    C. it is part of specialized vocabulary

    D. it is an unfamiliar word

    E. he is proud of the information

11. It is implied that Mr Hutchins

    A. is a gardener by occupation

    B. is a man of short stature

C. uses words cleverly

D. has a rich and varied vocabulary

E. is limited in his use of words

12. The expression 'on purely mechanical lines' (line 35) means that the conversation
    A. was entirely predictable
    B. was concerned with technical details
    C. was typical of the class of the Hutchins
    D. was aimless
    E. was polite but stilted

13. George Hutchins tried to avoid introducing Charles to his parents because
    A. he did not like Charles
    B. Charles was sorry for them
    C. he did not want to be interrupted
    D. he was ashamed of them
    E. they were bewildered

14. Some of the following information about George Hutchins is given in the passages:
    (i) He was a snob.
    (ii) He looked like his parents.
    (iii) He was decent and kindly.
    (iv) He was working class in appearance.
    (v) He was successful.
    Is it
    A. (i), (ii), (iii)?
    B. (iii), (iv), (v)?
    C. (i), (iii), (v)?
    D. (ii), (iii), (iv)?
    E. (i), (ii), (v)?

15. The word 'raw' (line 56) implies an attitude which was
    A. ruthless
    B. sensitive
    C. rough
    D. prejudiced
    E. vindictive

16. The word 'cult' (line 56) could best be replaced by
  A. culture
  B. toleration
  C. pursuit
  D. obsession
  E. increase

17. The word 'spawned' (line 58) implies that George
  A. was one of a large family
  B. was born near the sea
  C. was a member of a working-class family
  D. felt spurned by his parents
  E. felt no affection for his parents

18. The word 'unreality' (line 59) suggests that George's diction was
  A. unnatural
  B. ineffective
  C. unbelievable
  D. ridiculous
  E. unsuccessful

19. The word 'diction' (line 60) could best be replaced by
  A. language
  B. accent
  C. vocabulary
  D. dialect
  E. dictation

20. 'Lockwood's donnish snivelling' suggests that Lockwood was
  A. miserable
  B. snobbish
  C. affected
  D. unhealthy
  E. ridiculous

21. 'Stretched on the rack of his ludicrous predicament' (line 64) implies that Charles was
  A. unhappy
  B. in pain
  C. alert
  D. in difficulties
  E. exposed

22. When Charles spoke to Mr Hutchins he wanted
    A. to be friendly
    B. to sound casual
    C. to be rude
    D. to be funny
    E. to sound self-assured

23. The term 'brassily' (line 70) means that his words sounded
    A. loud
    B. hard
    C. empty
    D. rude
    E. bright

24. The main point of the description of the four men is that
    A. they are tough
    B. they are gamblers
    C. they are angry
    D. they are unfriendly
    E. they are unshaven

25. The word 'cowering' (line 78) is used in this context to imply that Charles is
    A. hiding
    B. cowardly
    C. unwell
    D. crouching down
    E. cramped for room

5

She watched him coming back from the gate, walking towards the slightly ornate suburban-style house she felt to be so incongruous set down on the bare rise, behind it the sheds and yards and the thin belt of shade trees. Yet he and his family were proud of it, grateful for its convenience and modernity, and had so clearly not understood her first quizzical remarks that she had never repeated them.

He stood on the edge of the veranda, and she saw in his face the anger that seemed to deepen because he knew the feeling to be impotent.   10

She said, 'What is it?'

'Mackay's two big tractors—that they were going to use for the scrub-clearing—they've been interfered with. Sand put into the oil. The one they started up will cost a few hundred to repair.'

'But no one would do that,' she said, as if already it were settled, her temporizing without point.

'We know who did it.'

Surely he didn't come right up to the sheds—as close as that to the house—'

'No. They left the tractors down in the bottom paddock. Where   20
they were going to start clearing.'

'And now—they can't?'

'Now they can't. Not till the tractor's repaired.'

She looked towards the distant line of the low scrub that was deepening in colour as the evening came. She said, 'That is what he wanted.'

'What he wants is to make as much trouble as he can. We haven't done anything to him.'

'You were going to clear the land along the bottom paddock at the back of Mackay's. Where he lives.'   30

'Where he lives?'

'You told me he lived in the bush there.'

'He lives anywhere. And he takes the ball floats off the taps in the sheep tank and the water runs to waste, and he breaks the fences when he feels like it, and leaves the gates open—'

'You think he does this deliberately?'

'How else?'

'Oh,' she said, 'yet it is all so ruthless.'

'You mean what he does?'

'No. You only ever think of what he does.' 40

'Well, I'll admit he's given us a few things to think about.'

'Clearing with those tractors and the chain,' she said. 'Everything in their path goes—kangaroos—all the small things that live in the scrub—all the trees—'

He looked at her as if her words held some relevance that must come to him. He said, 'We clear the land. Yes.'

'You clear it,' she said. 'It seems to be what is happening everywhere today.'

'I don't know what you mean, Ann,' he said.

She got up from the chair by the steps. 'Perhaps he feels some- 50 thing should be left.'

'Look,' he said, 'maybe you teach too much nature study at school. Or you read all this stuff about how we shouldn't shoot the bloody 'roos—so that when some crazy swine wrecks our property you think he's some sort of a—'

'Some sort of a what?'

'I don't know,' he said, aware she mocked him. 'Better than us.'

'No,' she said. 'Perhaps just different.'

'Different all right.'

'What are you going to do?' 60

'Get the police,' he said. 'They don't take much notice most of the time, but they will of this.' He looked at her as if he would provoke the calm he felt to be assumed. 'We'll burn him out if we can't get him any other way.'

She looked up quickly and for a moment he was afraid.

'You wouldn't do that.'

'He's gone too far this time,' he said stubbornly.

The long thin streamers of cloud above the darkening line of scrub were becoming deep and hard in colour, scarlet against the dying light. He watched her face that seemed now calm, remote, 70 as if her words were erased. She was small, slight, somehow always neat, contained. Her dark hair was drawn straight back, her brows clearly marked, lifting slightly so that they seemed to give humour sometimes to her serious expression, her firm mouth.

33

'I'd better go, Ken.'

'The family expect you for tea.'

'It's Sunday night. I've to work in the morning. I have some things to prepare.'

'Look,' he said. 'If it's this business—'

'No, I'm just tired. And I've assignments to mark.'

'All right,' he said.

As they drove she watched the long shadows that spread across the road and over the paddocks from the few shade trees, the light now with a clarity denied through the heat of the day. She would have liked to make some gesture to break the tension between them, to explain to him why she had been unwilling to stay and listen to the inevitable talk of what had happened. But to tell him that at such times she became afraid, as if she could never become one of them, certain that the disagreements now easily enough brought to a truce must in the end defeat them, would not lessen their dissension.

He said suddenly, 'You're worried about it, aren't you?'

She knew he referred to themselves, as if he had been aware of her own thoughts.

'Yes,' she said. 'Sometimes.'

'It could be all right, Ann. You'd come to like it here.'

'In so many ways I do.'

'It's nothing like it used to be. This light land has come good now. We've done well. We've got everything—you wouldn't be without anything you'd have in the city.'

'I know that, Ken,' she said.

'But you're not sure of it.'

She thought he perhaps did this deliberately, seeking to provoke an issue on material grounds, these at least being demonstrable of some conclusion, that he was lost, unwilling, in the face of their real uncertainty. He was more perceptive, she knew, than he cared to reveal, but he had a stubbornness she felt was perhaps impossible to defeat. Before it, she relented a little.

'Not sure of some things. You must give me time. After all, I— hadn't thought to live here. It's different for you.'

The few high trees stood out darkly above the low thick scrub, and beyond she could see the roofs of the town.

He said, 'This other business will probably be over next week, anyhow.'

She supposed he deliberately minimized this which perhaps he did not understand, preferring evasion, the pretence that when it was settled it would not matter. As to him it might not. But he was

34

so clearly afraid that she would escape. She reached out quickly
and touched his hand.

He stopped the car before the house near the end of the main 120
street, where she boarded. Farther down, near the club, she could
see the cars parked, and people moving without haste along the
pavements.

1. The woman feels the house to be incongruous because
    A. it is ornate
    B. the rise is bare
    C. it is behind the yards
    D. it does not suit the surroundings
    E. there are not enough trees to shade it

2. It is implied that the woman has
    A. said she does not like the house
    B. has made fun of the house
    C. has been very critical of the house
    D. has offended the family
    E. seems ungrateful to the family

3. The man appreciates the house because
    A. it has an interesting appearance
    B. it has good outbuildings
    C. it is easy to live in
    D. it is near the town
    E. it is on a hill

4. The man's anger seemed to deepen because
    A. the matter was out of his hands
    B. he was impotent
    C. it gave him satisfaction
    D. being angry would not solve the problem
    E. the woman did not share his feelings

5. The remark 'But no one would do that' (line 15) here implies
    A. she did not believe the man's statement
    B. she thought they did not know who had done it
    C. she thought a mistake had been made
    D. she realized who had done it
    E. she wanted to start an argument

6. When she says 'It is all so ruthless' (line 38) she refers to
   A. the clearing of the land by the tractors
   B. the behaviour of the man in the bush
   C. the attitude of her companion
   D. the living conditions in the bush
   E. the relationship of the people concerned

7. From the passage it is evident that concerning the man in the bush Ann and Ken
   A. both knew who he was
   B. had seen him on another occasion
   C. had spoken about him before
   D. had disagreed about his identity
   E. could not agree that he existed

8. The sentence 'He looked at her as if . . .' (line 45) implies that
   A. he did not think that she was serious
   B. he did not understand what she meant
   C. he expected more understanding from her
   D. he thought she was making fun of him
   E. he thought he ought to agree with her

9. Which of the following adjectives best describes Ann's opinion of the man in the bush?
   A. Superior.
   B. Crazy.
   C. Strange.
   D. Different.
   E. Sensitive.

10. It is implied (line 63) that Ken
    A. tried to assume a calm appearance
    B. thinks that Ann is being provocative
    C. believes that Ann is not as calm as she appears
    D. treats Ann with great respect
    E. is really afraid of the man in the bush

11. The word 'stubbornly' (line 67) relates to which of the following expressions which occur in the passage:
    A. She mocked him.
    B. He would provoke the calm.
    C. We'll burn him out.

36

D. He was afraid.

E. He's gone too far.

12. Ann is said to be all the following *except*

    A. short

    B. dark

    C. pretty

    D. neat

    E. slim

13. All the following words are used in a metaphorical sense *except*

    A. streamers

    B. deep

    C. hard

    D. scarlet

    E. dying

14. Their conversation is frequently abrupt and stilted. This indicates that they were

    A. excited

    B. uneasy

    C. embarrassed

    D. inarticulate

    E. angry

15. The expression 'the light now with a clarity denied through the heat of the day' means

    A. their misunderstanding was now over

    B. they now understood more clearly each other's point of view

    C. they had been angry and this clouded their understanding

    D. the countryside had been obscured by a heat-haze during the day

    E. the cool evening air sharpened their perception

16. Ann's ultimate fear was that

    A. she would disagree with Ken

    B. she would disagree with the family

    C. she would de defeated in argument

    D. she knew what would be discussed

    E. she would end her friendship with Ken

17. The expression 'seeking to provoke an issue on material grounds' (line 103) means that Ken was
    A. trying to start an argument about the land
    B. trying to reduce their disagreement to physical living conditions
    C. pointing out the improvements that he had carried out
    D. attempting to point out the benefits of living in that place
    E. trying to start an argument about the doubts expressed by Ann

18. The sentence beginning 'She thought he perhaps . . .' (line 103) suggests that Ann
    A. thinks that Ken did not know where they were
    B. thinks that Ken will not admit he is wrong
    C. thinks that Ken is trying to avoid the real cause of their doubts
    D. does not want to live without material benefits
    E. does not welcome Ken's attempts to influence her

19. The word 'perceptive' (line 106) could best be replaced by
    A. understanding
    B. receptive
    C. uncertain
    D. responsive
    E. emotional

20. Ann 'relented' (line 108) because
    A. she felt that Ken was uncertain
    B. Ken was perceptive
    C. Ken was stubborn
    D. she was worried
    E. she knew she could not win

21. The last but one paragraph beginning 'She supposed . . .' (line 115) Suggests that Ken
    A. was unintelligent
    B. preferred to argue
    C. pretended all was well
    D. avoided the issue
    E. was small-minded

6

When William was growing up, the family moved from the Bottoms to a house on the brow of the hill, commanding a view of the valley, which spread out like a convex cockleshell, or a clam-shell, before it. In front of the house was a huge old ash-tree. The west wind, sweeping from Derbyshire, caught the houses with full force, and the tree shrieked again. Morel liked it.

'It's music,' he said. 'It sends me to sleep.'

But Paul and Arthur and Annie hated it. To Paul it became almost a demoniacal noise. The winter of their first year in the new house their father was very bad. The children played in the street, on the brim of the wide, dark valley, until eight o'clock. Then they went to bed. Their mother sat sewing below. Having such a great space in front of the house gave the children a feeling of night, of vastness, and of terror. This terror came in from the shrieking of the trees and the anguish of the home discord. Often Paul would wake up, after he had been asleep a long time, aware of thuds downstairs. Instantly he was wide awake. Then he heard the booming shouts of his father, come home nearly drunk, then the sharp replies of his mother, then the bang, bang of his father's fist on the table, and the nasty snarling shout as the man's voice got higher. And then the whole was drowned in a piercing medley of shrieks and cries from the great, windswept ash-tree. The children lay silent in suspense, waiting for a lull in the wind to hear what their father was doing. He might hit their mother again. There was a feeling of horror, a kind of bristling in the darkness, and a sense of blood. They lay with their hearts in the grip of an intense anguish. The wind came through the tree fiercer and fiercer. All the cords of the great harp hummed, whistled, and shrieked. And then came the horror of the sudden silence, silence everywhere, outside and downstairs. What was it? Was it a silence of blood? What had he done?

39

The children lay and breathed the darkness. And then, at last, they heard their father throw down his boots and tramp upstairs in his stockinged feet. Still they listened. Then at last, if the wind allowed, they heard the water of the tap drumming into the kettle, which their mother was filling for morning, and they could go to sleep in peace.

So they were happy in the morning—happy, very happy playing, dancing at night round the lonely lamp-post in the midst of the darkness. But they had one tight place of anxiety in their hearts, one darkness in their eyes, which showed all their lives.

Paul hated his father. As a boy he had a fervent private religion.

'Make him stop drinking,' he prayed every night. 'Lord, let my father die,' he prayed very often. 'Let him not be killed at pit,' he prayed when, after tea, the father did not come home from work.

That was another time when the family suffered intensely. The children came from school and had their teas. On the hob the big black saucepan was simmering, the stew-jack was in the oven, ready for Morel's dinner. He was expected at five o'clock. But for months he would stop and drink every night on his way from work.

In the winter nights, when it was cold, and grew dark early, Mrs Morel would put a brass candlestick on the table, light a tallow candle to save the gas. The children finished their bread-and-butter, or dripping, and were ready to go out to play. But if Morel had not come they faltered. The sense of his sitting in all his pit-dirt, drinking, after a long day's work, not coming home and eating and washing, but sitting, getting drunk, on an empty stomach, made Mrs Morel unable to bear herself. From her the feeling was transmitted to the other children. She never suffered alone any more: the children suffered with her.

Paul went out to play with the rest. Down in the great trough of twilight, tiny clusters of lights burned where the pits were. A few last colliers struggled up the dim field-path. The lamplighter came along. No more colliers came. Darkness shut down over the valley; work was gone. It was night.

Then Paul ran anxiously into the kitchen. The one candle still burned on the table, the big fire glowed red. Mrs Morel sat alone. On the hob the saucepan steamed; the dinner-plate lay waiting on the table. All the room was full of the sense of waiting, waiting for the man who was sitting in his pit-dirt, dinnerless, some mile away from home, across the darkness, drinking himself drunk. Paul stood in the doorway.

'Has my dad come?' he asked.

'You can see he hasn't,' said Mrs Morel, cross with the futility of the question.

Then the boy dawdled about near his mother. They shared the same anxiety. Presently Mrs Morel went out and strained the potatoes.

'They're ruined and black,' she said; 'but what do I care?' 80

Not many words were spoken. Paul almost hated his mother for suffering because his father did not come home from work.

'What do you bother yourself for?' he said. 'If he wants to stop and get drunk, why don't you let him?'

'Let him!' flashed Mrs Morel. 'You may well say "let him."'

She knew that the man who stops on the way home from work is on a quick way to ruining himself and his home. The children were yet young, and depended on the breadwinner. William gave her the sense of relief, providing her at last with someone to turn to if Morel failed. But the tense atmosphere of the room on these wait- 90 ing evenings was the same.

1. The view from the houses could be described as
   A. a long and narrow valley
   B. a hilly plain
   C. a curved sea-shore
   D. a large dish-shaped valley
   E. a complex system of hills

2. The word 'shrieked' (line 6) is used to suggest that
   A. the tree was damaged
   B. the noise was deafening
   C. the wind was very strong
   D. the tree was very prominent
   E. the noise could be heard from afar

3. The word 'demoniacal' (line 9) means
   A. spiritual
   B. hellish
   C. ghostly
   D. devilish
   E. ghoulish

4. The phrase 'home discord' (line 15) refers to
   A. the parents' quarrelling
   B. children playing in the street

41

C. the sound of the wind
D. the noise of the tree
E. the space in front of the house

5. The 'terror' mentioned in (line 14) is explained in terms of
   A. feelings
   B. sounds
   C. suspense
   D. darkness
   E. isolation

6. The word 'medley' (line 21) could best be replaced by
   A. music
   B. symphony
   C. anguish
   D. mixture
   E. clash

7. 'A kind of bristling in the dark' (line 25) refers to
   A. a shuffling noise
   B. a brief struggle
   C. a prolonged whining sound
   D. something brushing past
   E. a presentment of fear

8. The sentence 'Was it a silence of blood?' (line 30) contains in its context all the following effects *except*
   A. contrast
   B. violence
   C. anticlimax
   D. uncertainty
   E. fear

9. The 'great harp' (line 28) refers metaphorically to
   A. the tree
   B. the wind
   C. their hearts
   D. the valley
   E. their fear

10. The children slept in peace only when
    A. the noise of the quarelling had died away
    B. they heard their father go to bed

C. the wind dropped and made less noise
D. they heard their mother filling the kettle
E. they could sense that morning was on its way

11. The effect of the children's experiences
   A. did not last long
   B. could be seen when morning came
   C. made them unhappy all the time
   D. lasted all their lives
   E. was worst at night

12. Paul's private religion is described as
   A. full of hate
   B. childish
   C. fiery
   D. without belief
   E. very strong

13. The impression that dominates the first two sentences of the paragraph beginning 'In the winter nights . . .' (line 52) is of
   A. darkness
   B. cold
   C. pleasure
   D. poverty
   E. light

14. The implications of the word 'sense' (line 56) could best be represented by
   A. feeling
   B. wisdom
   C. understanding
   D. idea
   E. fact

15. The statement that Mrs Morel was 'unable to bear herself' means that
   A. she sought other people's company
   B. she became physically weak
   C. she was very unhappy
   D. she was consumed with feelings of guilt
   E. she became very hungry

16. The expression 'trough of twilight' (line 62) is appropriate because
A. distances become blurred in the evening
B. it is an alliterative phrase
C. the valley becomes dark
D. the darkness seems to grow deeper
E. the evening is the time for food

17. Which of the following functions does the sentence 'It was night' (line 66) perform in the paragraph of which it is part?
A. It is a summary of the information.
B. It is the result of the events.
C. It is in contrast to the rest of the paragraph.
D. It is the climax of a sequence of events.
E. It gives the reason for the rest of the paragraph.

18. The scene in Mrs Morel's kitchen contains some of the following:
   (i) A brass candlestick.
   (ii) A glowing fire.
   (iii) An armchair marked with pit-dirt.
   (iv) A steaming saucepan.
   (v) A flickering gas-lamp.
Is it
A. (i), (ii), (iii)?
B. (i), (ii), (iv)?
C. (ii), (iv), (v)?
D. (ii), (iii), (iv)?
E. (i), (iii), (v)?

19. The word 'flashed' (line 85) reflects the feeling of which of the following words used shortly before in the passage?
A. Cross.
B. Futility.
C. Dawdled.
D. Anxiety.
E. Hated.

20. The 'breadwinner' (line 88) refers to
A. Mrs Morel
B. William
C. the colliery
D. Mr Morel
E. Paul

7

Prince Ali was an Egyptian, a near relation of the Khedive, who
had fled his country when the Khedive was deposed. He was a
bitter enemy of the English and was known to be actively engaged
in stirring up trouble in Egypt. The week before, the Khedive in
great secrecy had passed three days at the hotel and the pair of
them had held constant meetings in the Prince's apartments. He
was a little fat man with a heavy black moustache. He was living
with his two daughters and a certain Pasha, Mustapha by name,
who was his secretary and managed his affairs. The four of them
were now dining together; they drank a great deal of champagne,   10
but sat in a stolid silence. The two princesses were emancipated
young women who spent their nights dancing in restaurants with
the bloods of Geneva. They were short and stout, with fine black
eyes and heavy sallow faces; and they were dressed with a rich
loudness that suggested the Fish-market at Cairo rather than the
Rue de la Paix. His Highness usually ate upstairs but the princesses
dined every evening in the public dining-room: they were chaperoned vaguely by a little old Englishwoman, a Miss King, who
had been their governess; but she sat at a table by herself and they
appeared to pay no attention to her. Once Ashenden, going along   20
a corridor, had come upon the elder of the two fat princesses
berating the governess in French with a violence that took his
breath away. She was shouting at the top of her voice and suddenly
smacked the old woman's face. When she caught sight of Ashenden she gave a furious look and flinging into her room slammed
the door. He walked on as though he had noticed nothing.

On his arrival Ashenden had tried to scrape acquaintance with
Miss King, but she had received his advances not merely with
frigidity but with churlishness. He had begun by taking off his hat
when he met her, and she had given him a stiff bow, then he had   30

45

addressed her and she had answered with such brevity that it was evident that she wished to have nothing much to do with him. But it was not his business to be discouraged, so with what assurance he could muster he took the first opportunity to enter into conversation with her. She drew herself up and said in French, but with an English accent:

'I don't wish to make acquaintance with strangers.'

She turned her back on him and next time he saw her cut him dead.

She was a tiny woman, just a few little bones in a bag of wrinkled skin, and her face was deeply furrowed. It was obvious that she wore a wig, it was of a mousy brown, very elaborate and not always set quite straight, and she was heavily made up, with great patches of scarlet on her withered cheeks and brilliantly red lips. She dressed fantastically in gay clothes that looked as though they had been bought higgledy-piggledy from an old-clothes shop and in the day-time she wore enormous, extravagantly girlish hats. She tripped along in very small smart shoes with very high heels. Her appearance was so grotesque that it created consternation rather than amusement. People turned in the street and stared at her with open mouths.

Ashenden was told that Miss King had not been to England since she was first engaged as governess of the Prince's mother and he could not but be amazed to think of all she must have seen during those long years in the harems of Cairo. It was impossible to guess how old she was. How many of those short Eastern lives must have run their course under her eyes and what dark secrets must she have known! Ashenden wondered where she came from; an exile from her own country for so long, she must possess in it neither family nor friends: he knew that her sentiments were anti-English and if she had answered him so rudely he surmized that she had been told to be on her guard against him. She never spoke anything but French. Ashenden wondered what it was she thought of as she sat there, at luncheon and dinner by herself. He wondered if ever she read. After meals she went straight upstairs and was never seen in the public sitting-rooms. He wondered what she thought of those two emancipated princesses who wore garish frocks and danced with strange men in second-rate cafés. But when Miss King passed him on her way out of the dining-room it seemed to Ashenden that her mask of a face scowled. She appeared actively to dislike him. Her gaze met his and the pair of them looked at one another for a moment; he imagined that she tried to put into her stare an unspoken insult. It would have been pleasantly absurd in that painted, withered visage if it had not been for some reason rather oddly pathetic.

But now the Baroness de Higgins, having finished her dinner, gathered up her handkerchief and her bag, and with the waiters bowing on either side sailed down the spacious room. She stopped at Ashenden's table. She looked magnificent.

'I'm so glad you can play bridge tonight,' she said in perfect 80 English, with no more than a trace of German accent. 'Will you come to my sitting-room when you are ready and have your coffee?'

'What a lovely dress,' said Ashenden.

'It is frightful. I have nothing to wear, I don't know what I shall do now that I cannot go to Paris. Those horrible Prussians,' and her r's grew guttural as she raised her voice. 'why did they want to drag my poor country into this terrible war?'

She gave a sigh, and a flashing smile, and sailed on. Ashenden was among the last to finish and when he left the dining-room it 90 was almost empty. As he walked past Count Holzminden, Ashenden feeling very gay hazarded the shadow of a wink. The German agent could not be quite sure of it and if he suspected it might rack his brains to discover what mystery it portended. Ashenden walked up to the second floor and knocked at the baroness's door.

'*Entrez, entrez,*' she said and flung it open.

She took both his hands with cordiality and drew him into the room. He saw that the two persons who were to make the four had already arrived. They were Prince Ali and his secretary. Ash- 100 enden was astounded.

'Allow me to introduce Mr Ashenden to Your Highness,' said the baroness, speaking in her fluent French.

1. The Khedive was
   A. made a deputy
   B. assassinated
   C. promoted
   D. removed from power
   E. disgraced

2. In the metaphor 'stirring up trouble' the image refers to
   A. mixing a witch's brew.
   B. matter that had sunk to the bottom rising up
   C. the process of making liquid cool

47

D. the expenditure of effort in the process

E. the effect of an external force

3. The word 'emancipated' (line 11) means that the princesses were
   A. tired in appearance
   B. unattractive in character
   C. carefree in behaviour
   D. unrestricted in action
   E. unsophisticated in taste

4. The term 'chaperoned vaguely' suggests that Miss King was
   A. forgetful
   B. weak
   C. ineffectual
   D. strict
   E. fussy

5. The word 'berating' (line 22) here is most close in meaning to
   A. pushing
   B. hitting
   C. defying
   D. arguing
   E. scolding

6. The expression 'took his breath away' (line 22) signifies
   A. surprise
   B. violence
   C. shouting
   D. amazement
   E. fear

7. The use of words such as 'furious', 'flinging', 'slammed' suggests
   A. anger
   B. speed
   C. violence
   D. excitability
   E. scorn

8. The expression 'to scrape an acquaintance' (line 27) implies
   A. he did not like Miss King
   B. he bumped into Miss King
   C. he used any excuse to speak to Miss King

D. he wanted to become a close friend

E. he tried to find someone to introduce him

9. Miss King's behaviour to Ashenden could best be described as

A. unresponsive

B. rude

C. haughty

D. cool

E. indifferent

10. The expression 'cut him dead' (line 38) means that she

A. ignored him

B. attacked him

C. hoped he would die

D. interrupted him

E. offended him

11. All the following information about Miss King is true *except* that she

A. is small

B. is wizened

C. is bald

D. is made-up

E. is gaily-dressed

12. Which of the following statements about Miss King's appearance is true?

A. People laughed at her.

B. She was thought to be ugly.

C. People were alarmed when they saw her.

D. People pitied her.

E. She appeared to be untidy.

13. The word 'tripped' (line 48) here means that she

A. fell

B. stumbled

C. danced

D. ran

E. walked

14. It is suggested that the life of Eastern people is

A. exciting

B. mysterious

49

C. colourful
D. brief
E. varied

15. The phrase 'he could not but be amazed' is an example of
   A. indirect statement
   B. rhetorical speech
   C. exaggeration
   D. double negative
   E. ambiguity

16. The information given in the sentence beginning 'He wondered what she thought of those two ...' (line 66) suggests that the princesses
   A. were immoral
   B. lived exciting lives
   C. acted unlike other women
   D. had questionable taste
   E. were in disguise

17. The tone of the sentence beginning 'It would have been pleasantly absurd' (line 73) suggests that the attitude of the writer to Miss King is that he is
   A. making fun of her
   B. sorry for her
   C. insulting her
   D. indifferent towards her
   E. disgusted with her

18. Which of the following words used in the paragraph beginning 'But now ...' (line 76) most reflects the 'magnificence' of the Baroness de Higgins?
   A. Baroness.
   B. Gathered up.
   C. Bowing.
   D. Sailed.
   E. Spacious.

19. The use of the word 'hazarded' (line 92) implies that Ashenden was
   A. uncertain of the response
   B. feeling gay
   C. being cautious

D. familiar with the Count

E. unable to wink properly

20. The imagery in the expression 'rack his brains' refers to the process of

A. harming

B. hurting

C. stretching

D. storing

E. remembering

21. The word 'portended' (line 94) could best be replaced by

A. promised

B. implied

C. contained

D. reflected

E. opened

22. Some of the following information about the Baroness is given or implied in the passage.

  (i) She is a big woman.

 (ii) Her native language is German.

(iii) She is married to the Count Holzminden.

(iv) She is an actress.

 (v) She is a skillful linguist.

Is it

A. (i), (ii), (iii)?

B. (iii), (iv), (v)?

C. (i), (iii), (v)?

D. (i), (ii), (v)?

E. (ii), (iii), (iv)?

23. Ashenden was astounded to see Prince Ali and his secretary because

A. they did not speak to anyone

B. he did not expect them to play bridge

C. he thought they had been suspicious of him

D. he did not know they spoke English

E. they were at war with England

24. From the information in the passage it is most likely that Ashenden was

A. a teacher

B. a tourist

C. a businessman
D. a spy
E. a soldier

25. The action of the passage takes place in
   A. Cairo
   B. Paris
   C. Germany
   D. Geneva
   E. England

8

'Prisoner, what is your name?'

'As I am to lose it at daylight tomorrow morning, it is hardly worth concealing. Parker Adderson.'

'Your rank?'

'A somewhat humble one; commissioned officers are too precious to be risked in the perilous business of a spy. I am a sergeant.'

'Of what regiment?'

'You must excuse me; if I answer that it might, for anything I know, give you an idea of whose forces are in your front. Such knowledge as that is what I came into your lines to obtain, not to impart.'

'You are not without wit.'

'If you will have the patience to wait, you will find me dull enough tomorrow.'

'How do you know that you are to die tomorrow morning?'

'Among spies captured by night that is the custom. It is one of the nice observances of the profession.'

The general so far laid aside the dignity appropriate to a Confederate officer of high rank and wide renown as to smile. But no one in his power and out of his favour would have drawn any happy augury from that outward and visible sign of approval. It was neither genial nor infectious; it did not communicate itself to the other persons exposed to it—the caught spy who had provoked it and the armed guard who had brought him into the tent and now stood a little apart, watching his prisoner in the yellow candle-light. It was no part of that warrior's duty to smile: he had been detailed for another purpose. The conversation was resumed; it was, in fact, a trial for a capital offence.

'You admit, then, that you are a spy—that you came into my camp disguised as you are, in the uniform of a Confederate sol-

53

dier, to obtain information secretly regarding the numbers and disposition of my troops?'

'Regarding, particularly, their numbers. Their disposition I already knew. It is morose.'

The general brightened again; the guard, with a severer sense of his responsibility, accentuated the austerity of his expression and stood a trifle more erect than before. Twirling his grey slouch hat round and round upon his forefinger, the spy took a leisurely survey of his surroundings. They were simple enough. The tent was a common 'wall tent', about eight feet by ten in dimensions, lighted by a single tallow-candle stuck into the haft of a bayonet, which was itself stuck into a pine-table, at which the general sat, now busily writing and apparently forgetful of his unwilling guest. An old rag-carpet covered the earthen floor; an older hair-trunk, a second chair, and a roll of blankets were about all else that the tent contained; in General Clavering's command, Confederate simplicity and penury of 'pomp and circumstance' had attained their highest development. On a large nail driven into the tent-pole at the entrance was suspended a sword-belt supporting a long sabre, a pistol in its holster, and, absurdly enough, a bowie knife. Of that most unmilitary weapon it was the general's habit to explain that it was a cherished souvenir of the peaceful days when he was a civilian.

It was a stormy night. The rain cascaded upon the canvas in torrents, with the dull, drum-like sound familiar to dwellers in tents. As the whooping blasts charged upon it the frail structure shook and swayed and strained at its confining stakes and ropes.

The general finished writing, folded the half sheet of paper, and spoke to the soldier guarding Adderson: 'Here, Tassman, take that to the adjutant-general; then return.'

'And the prisoner, general?' said the soldier, saluting, with an inquiring glance in the direction of that unfortunate.

'Do as I said,' replied the officer curtly.

The soldier took the note and ducked himself out of the tent. General Clavering turned his handsome, clean cut face toward the Federal spy, looked him in the eyes, not unkindly, and said: 'It is a bad night, my man.'

'For me, yes.'

'Do you guess what I have written?'

'Something worth reading, I dare say. And—perhaps it is my vanity—I venture to suppose that I am mentioned in it.'

'Yes; it is a memorandum for an order to be read to the troops at *reveille* concerning your execution. Also some notes for the

54

guidance of the provost-marshal in arranging the details of that event.'

'I hope, general, the spectacle will be intelligently arranged, for I shall attend it myself.'

'Have you any arrangements of your own that you wish to make? Do you wish to see a chaplin, for example?' 80

'I could hardly secure a longer rest for myself by depriving him of some of his.'

'Good God, man! Do you mean to go to your death with nothing but jokes upon your lips? Do you not know that this is a serious matter?'

'How can I know that? I have never been dead in all my life. I have heard that death is a serious matter, but never from any of those who have experienced it.'

The general was silent for a moment; the man interested, perhaps amused, him—a type not previously encountered. 90

1. Officers were not employed as spies because the job was
   A. humble
   B. distasteful
   C. deceitful
   D. risky
   E. specialized

2. The expression 'for anything I know' (line 9) signifies that the prisoner
   A. is concealing what he knows
   B. knows all there is to know
   C. is uncertain of some information
   D. does not know the effect of his statements
   E. is ready to exchange information for his own benefit

3. The sentence 'You are not without wit' is an example of
   A. understatement
   B. comparative speech
   C. paradox
   D. exaggeration
   E. personification

4. A 'nice observance of the profession' (line 18) means that it is
   A. a closely-guarded secret
   B. an accepted treatment

55

C. an enjoyable experience
D. a way of recognizing spies
E. concerned with honourable behaviour

5. The word 'impart' (line 12) could best be replaced by
   A. discover
   B. inform
   C. reveal
   D. analyse
   E. depart

6. The implication of the words 'you will find me dull enough to-morrow' is that
   A. it will be a long night
   B. he is afraid
   C. the general's judgment will differ
   D. he will be dead
   E. he is not normally witty

7. Confederate officers of high rank were expected to be
   A. renowned
   B. witty
   C. happy
   D. powerful
   E. dignified

8. An 'augury' (line 22) is concerned with
   A. a message
   B. food and drink
   C. power
   D. the future
   E. a conclusion

9. The 'outward and visible sign' (line 22) referred to is his
   A. uniform
   B. smile
   C. rank
   D. dignity
   E. signature

10. The general's smile is described by comparing it to
    A. a disease
    B. a genius

C. a proof
D. a signal
E. a letter

11. The guard is described as a warrior because he is
    A. armed
    B. a soldier
    C. a guard
    D. at war
    E. brave

12. The prisoner's offence
    A. involved a great deal of money
    B. was appreciated by his own side
    C. took place in the main street
    D. was punishable by death
    E. was skilfully executed

13. Some of the following information about the spy is indicated in
    the passage.
      (i) He was in uniform.
     (ii) He wished to know the numbers of the troops.
    (iii) He wished to examine the morale of the soldiers.
    (iv) He wanted to know where the troops were distributed.
    Is it
    A. (i) and (ii)?
    B. (iii) and (iv)?
    C. (i) and (iii)?
    D. (ii) and (iv)?
    E. (ii) and (iii)?

14. The guard's sense of responsibility made him
    A. walk up and down faster
    B. speak with a firmer accent
    C. look more severe than before
    D. give orders in a fierce manner
    E. act in a correct military way

15. The spy's reaction to his situation and surroundings could best
    be described as
    A. uninterested
    B. nonchalent
    C. aggressive

D. lazy

E. uncooperative

16. The image typical of the Confederate ideals suggests an attitude of
   A. pomp and ceremony
   B. poverty
   C. makeshift
   D. severity and austerity
   E. simplicity and lack of ceremony

17. The phrase 'absurdly enough' is used because
   A. the weapons are hung on a nail
   B. the bowie knife is small
   C. the pistol is in its holster
   D. the bowie knife is not a military weapon
   E. there is too great a variety of weapons

18. The use of the verb 'cascaded' is appropriate because
   A. it is concerned with water
   B. the rain is noisy
   C. it concerns a violent motion
   D. the rain sounds like drums
   E. it is concerned with the noise of guns

19. The term 'whooping blasts' describes
   A. the enemy
   B. gunfire
   C. the rain
   D. the wind
   E. the tent

20. The implication of the word 'curtly' is that the officer
   A. does not waste words
   B. is pointing out the difference in rank
   C. has no time to be polite
   D. does not wish to discuss the prisoner
   E. has sympathy for the prisoner

9

There were many towns named Stratford in England, but the one that stood on the banks of the river Avon had special reason to be proud of its native sons. John of Stratford had became Archbishop of Canterbury and lay buried in a tomb of alabaster at the high alter, and Hugh Clopton had gone to the great city of London and ended by becoming its Lord Mayor.

By the middle of the sixteenth century these special glories were a thing of the past. But the stone bridge over the Avon that Sir Hugh Clopton had built at great expense for his native town had opened up a year-round traffic with London, and Stratford had become a thriving market community and was now one of the largest towns in Warwickshire. When the young men who were born in the near-by villages decided that they did not want to be farmers, they migrated to Stratford to learn a trade and settle down in one of its well-travelled streets.

Among the young men of Warwickshire who felt the pull of Stratford was one named John Shakespeare. John lived in the pleasant little village of Snitterfield, four miles to the north. His father was a tenant farmer and his brother was a tenant farmer, but John had no intention of following in their footsteps. When he left Snitterfield he probably had no higher ambition than to become a successful business man in Stratford; but before John Shakespeare died he had achieved the highest political office in town, and had been a justice of the peace, a landowner and a gentleman with a coat of arms. He had also become the father of a son named William who had a considerable success on the London stage; and, while this was not in itself a very dignified achievement from the Stratford point of view, John Shakespeare had the satisfaction of knowing before he died that his son was already investing his money in Stratford real estate.

The trade that young John Shakespeare selected for himself

was that of making gloves. Everyone wore gloves in the sixteenth century, and since their native manufacture was protected by Act of Parliament, it was a profitable trade. The glovers were one of the most powerful trade groups in Stratford, and on market days they put up their booths and trestles in the most strategic location in town. They did their selling just under the big clock in the paved market square, where most of the customers gathered, and it was not until more than a hundred years later that another powerful trade group, the mercers, managed to take this location away from them. John Shakespeare was a 'whittawer', a dealer in the fine white leather from which the best products were made, but like most of his fellow townsmen he sold other commodities, from timber to wool, in his spare time.

The Stratford that John Shakespeare knew was still a medieval town. It had never been walled, which accounted for its unusually straight and broad streets, but in spirit it was a tight, narrow little medieval community. Like every other town in England, Stratford was run on a strict, paternalistic system that had worked well for the citizens' remote ancestors and might be expected to work equally well for them. Every effort was made to protect local industry and keep away outsiders, all trade was strictly controlled and supervised, and every resident was hedged about with rules designed to keep himself and the town in order. An inhabitant of Stratford was fined if he let his dog go unmuzzled, if his duck wandered, if he played cards 'or any other unlawful games', if his children were not at home by eight o'clock in the summertime, if he failed to sweep his gutters or if he borrowed gravel from the town gravel pits. If he wanted to bring an outsider into his house he had to have a special licence from the High Bailiff, and if from a sense of compassion he gave shelter in his home to 'any strange woman' who was pregnant he was heavily fined.

The natural result of Stratford's strict medieval standards of conduct was that the men of Stratford's governing body were continually obliged to fine themselves and their fellow townsmen for breaking the rules. With so many rules to be enforced it was impossible to avoid breaking a few of them, and there was no citizen of Stratford so virtuous or so distinguished that he escaped a fine for one offence or another.

1. The 'glories' are described as 'special' (line 7) because
   A. Stratford was proud of them
   B. the people became important
   C. their sons lived in Stratford
   D. the events happened in Stratford
   E. the people were born in Stratford

2. Stratford became a thriving community because
   A. Sir Hugh Clopton was Lord Mayor of London
   B. it was the largest town in Warwickshire
   C. young men came into the town
   D. it produced famous men
   E. it had constant trade with London

3. The word 'migrated' (line 14) here means that
   A. the young men had a long journey
   B. they moved against their will
   C. they wished to live permanently in town
   D. the move was due to an impulse
   E. the move was only a temporary one

4. From the passage, none of the following statements can be justified
   except
   A. John Shakespeare's father was unsuccessful.
   B. John Shakespeare's father owned a farm.
   C. John Shakespeare was persuaded to go to Stratford.
   D. John Shakespeare's father saw his success.
   E. John Shakespeare did not want to be a farmer.

5. We learn all the following information about John Shakespeare
   except
   A. he held high office in the town
   B. he bore a coat of arms
   C. he owned land
   D. he had a large family
   E. he was a justice of the peace

6. William Shakespeare pleased his father because
   A. he bought property in Stratford
   B. he was a successful playwright
   C. he went to London
   D. he was an actor
   E. he knew how to make good investments

7. The term 'real estate' (line 30) refers to
   A. property not inherited
   B. business
   C. land
   D. successful speculation
   E. goods

8. The gloves worn in sixteenth-century England
   A. were an example of native art
   B. were not made very well
   C. cost a great deal to buy
   D. could not be imported
   E. were sold by Act of Parliament

9. The glovers' location was most 'strategic' (line 36) because it was
   A. most expensive
   B. under the clock
   C. where most customers gathered
   D. in the paved market-place
   E. carefully planned

10. The word 'location' (line 36) could best be replaced here by
   A. place
   B. site
   C. locality
   D. stand
   E. space

11. Stratford had straight and broad streets because
   A. it had no town walls
   B. it was a medieval town
   C. it was a busy market town
   D. it had a fine bridge
   E. it was a thriving community

12. The system is called 'paternalistic' (line 49) because
   A. it was an hereditary one
   B. the officials were referred to as town fathers
   C. the town was ruled by old men
   D. it treated the community as a family
   E. no women were allowed to hold office

13. In the passage it is implied that the town system of government
   A. was remote from the ordinary citizens
   B. was respected because it was the work of ancestors
   C. had been in existence a long time
   D. was unpopular with the people
   E. was specially suitable for Stratford

14. The image contained in the phrase 'hedged about' (line 53) implies a sense of
   A. interference
   B. restriction
   C. protection
   D. growth
   E. evasion

15. The use of the word 'designed' (line 54) in connection with rules suggests
   A. the rules were complicated
   B. the authors of the rules were cunning
   C. the rules were sketched out without detail
   D. the rules were on view for all to see
   E. the rules had been carefully planned

16. The words 'or any other unlawful games' (line 56) are in inverted commas because
   A. they are not to be taken seriously
   B. they refer only to trivial matters
   C. they are meant to be humorous
   D. they are a quotation from the rules
   E. they are an illustration of games like cards

17. The word 'borrowed' (line 58) implies all the following *except*
   A. took
   B. stole
   C. helped himself
   D. bought
   E. removed

18. The 'result' (line 63) is described as natural because
   A. the conduct was medieval
   B. the rules were medieval
   C. the Stratford people were unruly

D. there were too many rules

E. they wanted the fines from prosecution

19. The governing body of Stratford in their enforcement of laws could best be described as

A. strict

B. impartial

C. virtuous

D. hypocritical

E. unscrupulous

20. Which of the following statements about Stratford would seem to be the most accurate?

A. It had not changed since medieval times.

B. It was a thriving modern community.

C. The people were lawless and unscrupulous.

D. It was determined to look after local interests.

E. Its inhabitants had little regard for hygiene.

10

It was nine years since Ben had written for the theatre, but now, his pleasanter occupation gone, he returned to his old trade philosophically enough and with sturdy good humour. A novel kind of roguery had providentially appeared in London—the commercial possibility of newspapers had been discovered—and to this invitation he energetically responded with *The Staple of News*.

Admitting first of all the prime importance of a busy inquisitive restless temper in the age, there were three people mainly responsible for the birth of periodic journalism. One was the Queen of Bohemia, another was a stationer called Nathaniel Butter, and the third was Captain Gainsford, a veteran of the Irish Wars. Elizabeth of Bohemia was London's darling and when her kingdom was stolen by the detestable armies of Spain, European politics became a matter of poignant interest. For some time the chief source of news was Amsterdam, and the Dutch bulletins were so sensational that they greatly stimulated England's thirst for information without wasting time on educating its palate to the taste of authenticity. By 1623, however, the Amsterdam monopoly was broken, and a weekly news-sheet was published from Pope's Head Alley whose reckless omniscience compared very favourably with the encyclopaedic assurance of Holland.

Butter had already shown his enterprise by publishing *King Lear*, a pamphlet protesting against Dutch boats fishing in English waters, part of Chapman's *Homer*, and the account of an interesting murder in Yorkshire; while Gainsford had written a life of the Earl of Tyrone, and a gossiping account of England's natural superiority to all other countries. The Captain had travelled far and wide, and wrote with the authority of one to whom the Golden Horn was familiar, the Grand Canal a friendly waterway. He was an admirable man for Butter's purpose, for he had an easy prolific pen and the proper courage of a soldier. Sitting in his room in Pope's Head Ally he conquered towns, crossed the Rhine, invaded provinces, repelled a flank attack, and with unfailing aplomb made history of dubious inference. The *Weekly Courant* became very popular.

Gainsford and Butter had genius. They knew when the iron was hot, and they knew how to strike it. But Ben's genius was rarely tactful, and he failed to remember, or did not trouble to consider, that pouring cold water on a red-hot surface causes a violent reaction. He played a cheerful hose on a glowing occasion for satire, and the result was a lot of very angry vapour.

The third act of Ben's comedy showed a newspaper office conducted by a staff that included an unmistakable caricature of Butter, a barber, a court parasite, and one or two other semi-professional gossips. Distinguished visitors arrive, and are treated to samples of the day's latest news. They are told that the King of Spain has been elected Pope, that Galileo has invented a fatal ray to burn up enemy shipping, and the Dutch possess a mechanical eel for submarine warfare. Then the office is invaded by a throng of Puritan customers eager for ecclesiastical news, and they are told, for sixpence an item or so, that the coming of the prophet Baal is now momentarily expected, and that the Grand Turk will shortly celebrate his conversion to Christianity by a visit to the Reformed Church in Amsterdam. All this was good hilarious travesty, of the *Courant*'s pages. Today it may seem wild travesty, but actually it was too close and pointed. Most of the audience did not quite recognize the burlesque and were angrily unsure how much they were meant to believe. Nathaniel's stage-news sounded so very like Butter's Pope's Head Alley news, and yet. . . . The King of Spain might perhaps be elected Pope, and his general Spinola made commander of the Jesuits—anything about Jesuits was credible—but they refused to believe in the Dutch submarine. Jonson, they concluded, was gulling them, deliberately inventing falsehoods, fooling them and filling them with fraudulent information. They became indignant. Their virgin credulity was being outraged. They shouted, they protested, they interrupted the impertinent scene. And when the play was published Ben found it necessary to prefix an explanation that the 'news' in it was not meant to be real news, but only burlesque of *Courant* news.

1. The 'old trade' referred to in line 2 is
   A. teaching philosophy
   B. laying bricks
   C. fighting professionally
   D. acting as a comedian
   E. writing plays

2. The adverb 'providentially' (line 4) implies that events were
   A. unexpected
   B. taking a turn for the better
   C. were of benefit to Ben Jonson
   D. were concerned with commerce
   E. were of benefit to rogues

3. From the information given in the passage, *The Staple of News* is
   A. a play
   B. a newspaper
   C. a novel
   D. a poem
   E. a magazine

4. The word 'temper' (line 9) could best be replaced by
   A. anger
   B. feeling
   C. disagreement
   D. enquiry
   E. revolt

5. The main reason for the start of newspapers was that
   A. people were angry about conditions of living
   B. it had the backing of royalty
   C. a publisher was prepared to support the venture
   D. people were anxious to get news
   E. it was an age of political unrest

6. The use of words such as 'darling', 'stolen', 'detestable', 'poignant' suggests that this writing was
   A. exaggerated
   B. descriptive
   C. objective
   D. critical
   E. emotive

7. England's 'thirst for information' (line 17) is described
   A. in an exaggerated style
   B. with reference to Dutch bulletins
   C. by comparison with sensational news
   D. by using extended metaphor
   E. in terms of paradox

8. The English enjoyed the Dutch news because
   A. they were anxious to be educated
   B. it was sensational
   C. they did not question its accuracy
   D. they wanted news from Europe
   E. it was about food and drink

9. The tone of the paragraph beginning 'Butter had already shown. . .' (line 23) could best be described as
   A. intellectual
   B. sarcastic
   C. humorous
   D. academic
   E. informative

10. It is implied that English reporters
   A. knew a great deal
   B. were fearless in getting news
   C. pretended to know a great deal
   D. were more confident than those in Holland
   E. relied on references from Dutch books

11. Butter's publications could best be described as
   A. learned
   B. sensational
   C. patriotic
   D. topical
   E. catholic

12. It is implied that Captain Gainsford was
   A. a stylistic writer
   B. a man of imagination
   C. a brave soldier
   D. an accurate reporter
   E. a writer of scandal

13. The word 'aplomb' (line 34) could best be replaced by
    A. regularity
    B. self-assurance
    C. insolence
    D. punctuality
    E. courage

14. It is suggested that Ben Jonson's satire was
    A. ill-directed and inaccurate
    B. foolish and careless
    C. timely but unpopular
    D. a badly performed experiment
    E. difficult to judge by results

15. It is implied that part of a barber's job was
    A. to act as a reporter
    B. to work on a newspaper
    C. to amuse
    D. to gossip
    E. to work at court

16. The 'samples of the day's latest news' (line 47) could best be described as
    A. amusing
    B. ludicrous
    C. prophetic
    D. provocative
    E. exciting

17. The contrast in attitude to Jonson's 'news' then and now is reflected in which of the following pairs?
    A. trevesty : burlesque
    B. hilarious : wild
    C. close : pointed
    D. play : audience
    E. staff : customers

18. The words 'and yet . . .' (line 60) imply that
    A. the audience was unused to burlesque
    B. the news did not agree with other sources
    C. the audience was not sure if the news was true
    D. a passage has been omitted from the original
    E. there is a change of emphasis in the subject matter

19. The vigour of the audience's reaction to Ben Jonson's play is reflected in the passage by the use of
A. violent verbs
B. vivid images
C. imaginative vocabulary
D. unusual punctuation
E. sentence structure

20. Their 'credulity' is described as 'virgin' (line 66) because it was
A. pure
B. weak
C. feminine
D. untried
E. outraged

11

Observation. It might be argued with unanswerable cogency that all methods of scientific inquiry involve observation. Of course they do. The point of including it here is to contrast cases in which observation of 'real life' situations is the method adopted, with cases in which some kind of experimental control is used. In social-psychological research into life in a village, a factory, a housing estate, or a hospital the whole point is to find out what is happening with the minimum disturbance introduced by the investigator. He must disturb the situation somehow by his questioning, interviewing, and form-filling, but this can be reduced by what is sometimes called 'participant observation' when he makes some attempt at melting into the scene by becoming a factory hand, a resident, or a nurse.

The position of the social scientist in the process of observing is frequently discussed. It is complained that he has no accepted role except the invidious one of 'snooper'. In America people seem to be more amenable to being watched and investigated than they are in Britain, where the social scientist is liable to be suspect. This means that elaborate precautions have to be taken beforehand, and the prestige of any parties who are likely to be ruffled if they are not told beforehand must be safeguarded; the conflicting interests of industrialists and Trade Unionists must be considered when research of this kind is carried out in the industrial field; the suspicions of operatives and housewives must be lulled to rest; the goodwill of all officials must be delicately courted. Professor Simey has put the problem as one of 'getting in, staying in, and getting out'. Once the observer has 'got in', he must obviously win such confidence as will enable him to stay there. This is clearly more easy when the subject of his research is connected with an issue, such as housing or easing difficult human relations, which the subjects of his research have at heart. It is harder when they

71

are quite mystified by the questions they are asked. Because of this, a little subterfuge is not unknown here and there. On the other hand, if the matter of inquiry is one of burning interest, or if the subjects of the inquiry have become themselves interested in the research, can the social scientist just snap his files together when he has got all the information he wants, and march off? The subjects may feel that they have been led up the garden path, betrayed, used as guinea-pigs, and so forth. Extraction from the scene of investigation for the sensitive scientist is often a delicate matter, particularly when he remembers that the reputation of his subject, which anyway is rather dubious, is at stake. 40

With all these difficulties it is not surprising that so much social research centres round school-children and criminals; both categories of persons are accessible and neither is likely to complain.

Experiment. The function of experiment in scientific research is to produce a controlled situation in which the factors thought to be relevant to the effect which is being investigated can be varied in 50 turn, the others being kept constant. By this means the influence of each variable can be studied, and the results generalized to apply to situations outside the laboratory. In the physical sciences the problem is fairly straightforward, though the technique employed may be extremely complicated. The material with which the physical scientist is dealing does not resist manipulation, though it may be difficult to manipulate, it does not change its nature in the presence of the experimenter himself, and he, in turn, can be pretty certain that the phenomena he studies in his laboratory are no different from the phenomena outside in the real world. 60 The social scientist is in a very different position. In human behaviour we know that intellectual ability, mood, personal background, and personal aims and interests are all relevant, and that everyone is different from everyone else; the complete control of all relevant factors is impossible. To get round this you may have to use a large number of subjects or groups, and repeat the experiment a number of times, in the hope that personal and ephemeral differences will cancel out.

1. The cogency is 'unanswerable' (line 1) because
    A. there is no answer
    B. the answer is not yet known
    C. there is no argument

72

D. the inquiry is not finished
E. there is not enough time to answer

2. The control is called 'experimental' (line 5) because
   A. it is in its early stages
   B. it concerns new ideas
   C. it is carried out in laboratories
   D. it concerns experiments
   E. it involves research

3. In social-psychological research, the investigator must do his job
   A. with great concern for detail
   B. with as little disturbance as possible
   C. without becoming too involved
   D. by questioning people
   E. by taking a menial job

4. The use of the word 'melting' (line 12) implies that the investigator should be
   A. unobtrusive
   B. kindly
   C. cooperative
   D. flexible
   E. active

5. The word 'invidious' (line 16) could best be replaced by
   A. enviable
   B. recognized
   C. secret
   D. hateful
   E. universal

6. It is suggested that American people are
   A. more patient than those of Britain
   B. are readier to cooperate than British people
   C. more easily annoyed than the British
   D. get on better with each other than the British
   E. are more used to being observed

7. In the passage it states that the 'prestige of the parties'
   A. should be protected
   B. is a political matter
   C. is the main concern of the social scientist

73

D. may be a cause of danger

E. creates suspicion of the social-scientist

8. The use of the phrase 'conflicting interests' suggests that the industrialists and the Trade Unions

A. do not agree with each other

B. are concerned with money matters

C. will always be irritated by the social scientist

D. represent opposing points of view

E. will be willing to join in experiments

9. The phrase 'lulled to rest' (line 24) implies a comparison with

A. sleep

B. laziness

C. work

D. storm

E. music

10. Issues will be easier to research if

A. they concern the subjects' emotions

B. they are sympathetic to the people

C. the subjects feel deeply about them

D. the subjects are not difficult people

E. they concern the subjects' relations

11. The word 'subterfuge' (line 33) can best be replaced by

A. preparation

B. cunning

C. bribery

D. deceit

E. explanation

12. The term 'subjects of the inquiry' refers to

A. the matters being investigated

B. the people being investigated

C. the people doing the investigation

D. the people who are indignant about the investigation

E. the facts revealed by an inquiry

13. The use of the term 'snap his files together' (line 36) here suggests

A. finality

B. indiscretion

C. insensitivity

D. cleverness

E. decision

14. The comparison with 'guinea-pigs' (line 38) is appropriate because guinea-pigs
    A. are small and inoffensive
    B. are often kept in restricted conditions
    C. are not required to look after themselves
    D. are often used in scientific experiments
    E. have no control over their environment

15. The reputation referred to in (line 41) belongs to
    A. the people investigated
    B. the social scientist
    C. the cause of investigation
    D. social science itself
    E. the places where research is done

16. Which of the following statements can be justified from the passage?
    A. Social scientists have to be sensitive people.
    B. The work of social scientists often affects their health.
    C. Some social scientists find it difficult to withdraw from an investigation.
    D. Social scientists can sometimes destroy reputations where they hold investigations.
    E. To draw conclusions from an investigation is difficult for the social scientist.

17. In the passage it is implied that
    A. the social scientist is still justifying his work
    B. the social scientist is handling highly confidential material
    C. the social scientist persuades people to betray themselves
    D. the social scientist investigates people of doubtful character
    E. the character of some social scientists is unsatisfactory

18. The word 'accessible' (line 45) means
    A. ready to question
    B. unable to get away
    C. suitable for experiment
    D. easy to get at
    E. of undeveloped mentality

19. The sentence beginning the section entitled *'Experiment'* (line 48) essentially is about
A. the function of experiment in scientific research
B. the production of a controlled situation
C. the relevance of the factors concerned
D. the effects being investigated
E. the variation and constancy of various factors

20. Some of the following statements are made about the work of the physical scientist.
  (i) He can organize his material as he wishes.
 (ii) Conditions in the laboratory are different from the world outside.
(iii) The character of the scientist does not affect the work.
(iv) The scientist does not affect the material he works with.
Is it
A. (i) and (ii)?
B. (iii) and (iv)?
C. (ii) and (iii)?
D. (i) and (iv)?
E. (i) and (iii)?

21. The work of the social scientist is made difficult because
A. it is different from that of the physical scientist
B. people's intellectual ability varies
C. the relevant aims and interests are hard to define
D. no two people are alike
E. the relevant statistics are hard to control

22. 'Ephemeral' differences (line 67) are those which depend on
A. character
B. place
C. disease
D. time
E. nationality

23. From the tone and style of this passage, it can be assumed that it was written
A. for social scientists
B. for scientists in general
C. for the general reader
D. as part of an official enquiry
E. as a document for recruiting social scientists

76

12

A

The glory of the beauty of the morning—
The cuckoo crying over the untouched dew;
The blackbird that has found it, and the dove
That tempts me on to something sweeter than love;
White clouds ranged even and fair as new-mown hay;
The heat, the stir, the sublime vacancy
Of sky and meadow and forest and my own heart—
The glory invites me, yet it leaves me scorning
All I can ever do, all I can be,
Beside the lovely of motion, shape and hue,   10
The happiness I fancy fit to dwell
In beauty's presence. Shall I now this day
Begin to seek as far as heaven, as hell,
Wisdom or strength to match this beauty, start
And tread the pale dust pitted with small dark drops,
In hope to find whatever it is I seek,
Hearkening to short-lived happy-seeming things
That we know naught of, in the hazel copse?
Or must I be content with discontent
As larks and swallows are perhaps with wings?   20
And shall I ask at the day's end once more
What beauty is, and what I can have meant
By happiness? And shall I let all go,
Glad, weary, or both? Or shall I perhaps know
That I was happy oft and oft before,
Awhile forgetting how I am fast pent,
How dreary-swift, with naught to travel to,
Is Time? I cannot bite the day to the core.

1. The glory the poet speaks of could best be summarized as
   A. the beauty of bird-song
   B. the clouds floating in the sky
   C. sublime feelings of love
   D. the beauty of the morning
   E. the beauty of field and forest

2. The effect of the glory on the poet is to make him feel
   A. inspired
   B. inadequate
   C. happy
   D. sad
   E. wise

3. The words 'I fancy' (line 11) emphasize the poet's
   A. imagination
   B. hope
   C. doubt
   D. inspiration
   E. bitterness

4. In beauty's presence the poet expects to find beauty expressed in terms of all the following except:
   A. movement
   B. colour
   C. joy
   D. shape
   E. heaven

5. In his search to match the glory what does the poet expect to find?
   A. Wisdom.
   B. Strength.
   C. Sadness.
   D. Hope.
   E. He does not know.

6. Lines 17 and 18 refer to the ideas expressed in
   A. lines 2–3
   B. lines 7–8
   C. lines 12–13
   D. lines 21–23
   E. lines 24–26

78

7. At the end of the day the poet will have found
   A. beauty
   B. happiness
   C. weariness
   D. uncertainty
   E. forgetfulness

8. The mood of the poem could best be described as
   A. disillusion
   B. frustration
   C. bitterness
   D. resignation
   E. nostalgia

B

Only a man harrowing clods
In a slow silent walk
With an old horse that stumbles and nods
Half asleep as they stalk.

Only thin smoke without flame
Form the heaps of couch-grass;
Yet this will go onward the same
Though Dynasties pass.

Yonder a maid and her wight
Come whispering by: 10
War's annals will cloud into night
Ere their story die.

1. The words 'only' (line 1) and 'yet' are used to imply
   A. time
   B. a problem
   C. contrast
   D. movement
   E. a question

2. The point of the 'thin smoke' is that
   A. the fire is dying
   B. it has been raining
   C. the fire is carefully built
   D. the fire seems unimportant
   E. it is growing dark

3. 'Couch–grass' (line 6) is
   A. soft grass
   B. grass used for bedding
   C. grass that has been cut
   D. coarse grass
   E. dried grass

4. The word 'Dynasties' is written here with a capital letter because
   A. it is a proper noun
   B. it gives the word added importance
   C. it concerns rulers and royalty
   D. it is an unusal word
   E. it is a collective noun

5. The word 'wight' (line 9) means
   A. lover
   B. man
   C. companion
   D. confidant
   E. chaperone

6. The word 'whispering' (line 10) reflects the same idea as which of
   the following words from the first stanza?
   A. Harrowing.
   B. Slow.
   C. Silent.
   D. Nods.
   E. Stalk.

7. The word 'annals' (line 11) means
   A. records
   B. repetition
   C. atrocities
   D. legends
   E. terrors

8. The idea conveyed by the word 'night' could best be represented by
A. darkness
B. the past
C. void
D. oblivion
E. space

9. Which of the following literary ornaments helps to slow down the pace of the first stanza?
A. Rhyme.
B. Short words.
C. Country images.
D. Alliteration.
E. Lack of punctuation.

10. The point of the poem could best be expressed by which of the following sentences?
A. War is a terrible thing.
B. The most important thing in life is love.
C. Life is a boring experience.
D. The lasting things in life may seem trivial.
E. Nothing endures for ever.

13

I have lost my stick. That is the outstanding event of the day, for it is day again. The bed has not stirred. I must have missed my point of purchase, in the dark. *Sine qua non*, Archimedes was right. The stick, having slipped, would have plucked me from my bed if I had not let it go. It would of course have been better for me to relinquish my bed than to lose my stick. But I had no time to think. The fear of falling is the source of many a folly. It is a disaster. I suppose the wisest thing now is to live it over again, meditate upon it and be edified. It is thus that man distinguishes himself from the ape and rises, from discovery to discovery, ever higher, towards the light. Now that I have lost my stick I realize what it is I have lost and all it means to me. And thence ascend, painfully, to an understanding of the Stick, shorn of all its accidents such as I had never dreamt of. What a broadening of the mind. So that I half discern, in the veritable catastrophe that has befallen me, a blessing in disguise. How comforting that is. Catastrophe too in the ancient sense no doubt. To be buried in lava and not turn a hair, it is then a man shows what stuff he is made of. To know you can do better next time, unrecognizably better, and that there is no next time, and that it is a blessing there is not, there is a thought to be going on with. I thought I was turning my stick to the best possible account, like a monkey scratching its fleas with the key that opens its cage. For it is obvious to me now that by making more intelligent use of my stick I might have extracted myself from my bed and perhaps even got myself back into it, when tired of rolling and dragging myself about the floor or on the stairs. That would have introduced a little variety into my decomposition. How is it that never occurred to me?

It is true I had no wish to leave my bed. But can the sage have no wish for something the very possibility of which he does not conceive? I don't understand. The sage perhaps. But I? It is day again, at least what passes for such here. I must have fallen asleep after a brief bout of discouragement, such as I have not experienced for a long time. For why be discouraged, one of the thieves was saved, that is a generous percentage. I see the stick on the floor, not far from the bed. That is to say I see part of it, as of all one sees. It might just as well be at the equator, or one of the poles. No, not quite, for perhaps I shall devise a way of retrieving it, I am so ingenious. All is not then yet quite irrevocably lost.

1. The second sentence implies that
   A. the day has been full of incident
   B. every day is exciting
   C. the writer has slept badly
   D. there is a great deal of interest happening
   E. the loss is of great importance

2. Which of the following expresses best the meaning of the sentence beginning 'The fear of falling . . .' (line 7)?
   A. Man's instinct always protects him.
   B. Falling is the result of foolish behaviour.
   C. Man's timidity leads him into actions he will regret.
   D. It is foolish to be afraid of falling.
   E. Disaster is usually caused by folly.

3. The edification (line 9) will be that the writer will
   A. learn from experience
   B. find comfort
   C. regret his folly
   D. will remember only what he wants to
   E. pass the time away

4. The 'light' (line 11) could best be expressed as
   A. intelligence
   B. understanding
   C. heaven
   D. love
   E. civilization

5. The word 'Stick' (line 13) is written with a capital letter because
   A. it refers to one special stick
   B. it is a proper noun
   C. the stick has acquired a special significance

83

D. the stick was of great importance

E. it is the central theme of the passage

6. 'Shorn of all its accidents' (line 13) suggests that
   A. the writer frequently dropped the stick
   B. the stick was the cause of many accidents
   C. the accidents became clear to the writer
   D. the writer understood the real significance of the stick
   E. the writer had been involved in an accident

7. The ultimate judgment of the writer concerning the loss of his stick is that it is
   A. a disaster
   B. painful
   C. a benefit
   D. a catastrophe
   E. foolish

8. 'There is a thought to be going on with' refers to
   A. a disappointment
   B. an antithesis
   C. a paradox
   D. a forecast
   E. a memory

9. The comparison made in the sentence beginning 'I thought I was turning . . .' (line 21) is to show
   A. lack of intelligence
   B. wasted opportunity
   C. ignorance
   D. a sense of humour
   E. indifference

10. From the tone of the passage, which of the following is most likely to describe the writer?
    A. Religious.
    B. Old.
    C. Wise.
    D. Humorous.
    E. Mad.

11. The words 'But I' (line 30) imply that the writer
   A. does not wish to leave his bed
   B. does not understand the problem
   C. is not a wise person
   D. is uncertain of the future
   E. wishes to draw attention to himself

12. The reference to the crucifixion implies that the writer thought of himself as
   A. a thief
   B. a saviour
   C. a sinner
   D. a gambler
   E. a martyr

13. The point of the reference to the crucifixion is that
   A. one can find comfort in religion
   B. there is always room for hope
   C. crime does not always carry punishment
   D. all life is only a lottery
   E. faith will solve all problems

14. The point of the sentence beginning 'That is to say . . .' (line 35) could best be expressed as which of the following:
   A. The stick was partly hidden by the bed.
   B. One cannot see things easily when lying in bed.
   C. He knew the stick was there as he could see part of it.
   D. One cannot understand anything completely.
   E. One only sees what one wants to.

15. The style of this passage could best be described as
   A. terse
   B. dramatic
   C. vague
   D. descriptive
   E. repetitive

14

We landed, hauled up the boat, and then feebly sat down on our belongings to review the situation, and Maria came and shook herself over each of us in turn. We had run into a little cove, guided by the philanthropic beam of a candle in the upper window of a house about a hundred yards away. The candle still burned on, and the anaemic daylight exhibited to us our surroundings, and we debated as to whether we could at 2.45 a.m. present ourselves as objects of compassion to the owner of the candle. I need hardly say that it was the ladies who decided on making the attempt, having, like most of their sex, a courage incomparably superior to ours in such matters; Bernard and I had not a grain of genuine compunction in our souls, but we failed in nerve.

We trailed up from the cove, laden with emigrants' bundles, stumbling on wet rocks in the half-light, and succeeded in making our way to the house.

It was a small two-storeyed building, of that hideous breed of architecture usually dedicated to the rectories of the Irish Church; we felt that there was something friendly in the presence of a pair of carpet slippers in the porch, but there was a hint of exclusiveness in the fact that there was no knocker and that the bell was broken. The light still burned in the upper window, and with a faltering hand I flung gravel at the glass. This summons was appallingly responded to by a shriek; there was a flutter of white at the panes, and the candle was extinguished.

'Come away!' exclaimed Miss Shute, 'it's a lunatic asylum!'

We stood our ground, however, and presently heard a footstep within, a blind was poked aside in another window, and we were inspected by an unseen inmate; then someone came downstairs, and the hall door was opened by a small man with a bald head and a long sandy beard. He was attired in a brief dressing-gown, and on his shoulder sat, like an angry ghost, a large white cockatoo.

Its crest was up on end, its beak was a good two inches long and curved like a Malay kris; its claws gripped the little man's shoulder. Maria uttered in the background a low and thunderous growl.

'Don't take any notice of the bird, please,' said the little man nervously, seeing our united gaze fixed upon this apparition; 'he's extremely fierce if annoyed.'

The majority of our party here melted away to either side of the hall door, and I was left to do the explaining. The tale of our misfortunes had its due effect, and we were ushered into a small drawing-room, our host holding the door for us, like a nightmare footman with bare shins, a gnome-like bald head, and an unclean spirit swaying on his shoulder. He opened the shutters, and we sat decorously round the room, as at an afternoon party, while the situation was further expounded on both sides. Our entertainer, indeed, favoured us with the leading items of his family history, amongst them the facts that he was a Dr Fahy from Cork, who had taken somebody's rectory for the summer, and had been prevailed on by some of his patients to permit them to join him as paying guests.

'I said it was a lunatic asylum,' murmured Miss Shute to me.

'In point of fact,' went on our host, 'there isn't an empty room in the house, which is why I can only offer your party the use of this room and the kitchen fire, which I make a point of keeping burning all night.'

He leaned back complacently in his chair, and crossed his legs; then, obviously remembering his costume, sat bolt upright again. We owed the guiding beams of the candle to the owner of the cockatoo, an old Mrs Buck, who was, we gathered, the most paying of all the patients, and also obviously, the one most feared and cherished by Dr Fahy. 'She has a candle burning all night for the bird, and her door open to let him walk about the house when he likes,' said Dr Fahy; 'indeed, I must say her passion for him amounts to dementia. He's very fond of me, and Mrs Fahy's always telling me I should be thankful, as whatever he did we'd be bound to put up with it!'

Dr Fahy had evidently a turn for conversation that was unaffected by circumstances; the first beams of the early sun were lighting up the red chair covers before the door closed upon his brown dressing-gown, and upon the stately white back of the cockatoo, and the demoniac possession of laughter that had wrought in us during the interview burst forth unchecked. It was most painful and exhausting, as much laughter always is; but by far the most serious part of it was that Miss Sally, who was sitting in the window, somehow drove her elbow through a pane of glass, and Bernard, in pulling down the blind to conceal the damage, tore it off the roller.

There followed on this catastrophe a period during which reason tottered and Maria barked furiously. Philippa was the first to pull herself together, and to suggest an adjournment to the kitchen fire that, in honour of the paying guests, was never quenched, and, respecting the repose of the household, we proceeded thither with a stealth that convinced Maria we were engaged in a rat hunt. The boots of paying guests littered the floor, the debris of their last repast covered the table; a cat in some unseen fastness crooned a war song to Maria, who feigned unconsciousness and fell to scientific research in the scullery.

We roasted our boots at the range, and Bernard, with all a sailor's gift for exploration and theft, prowled in noisome purlieus and emerged with a jug of milk and a lump of salt butter. No one who has not been a burglar can at all realize what it was to roam through Dr Fahy's basement storey, with the rookery of paying guests asleep above, and to feel that, so far, we had repaid his confidence by breaking a pane of glass and a blind, and putting the scullery tap out of order. I have always maintained that there was something wrong with it before I touched it, but the fact remains that when I had filled Philippa's kettle, no human power could prevail upon it to stop flowing. For all I know to the contrary it is running still.

It was in the course of our furtive return to the drawing-room that we were again confronted by Mrs Buck's cockatoo. It was standing in malign meditation on the stairs, and on seeing us it rose, without a word of warning, upon the wing, and with a long screech flung itself at Miss Sally's golden-red head, which a ray of sunlight had chanced to illumine. There was a moment of stampede, as the selected victim, pursued by the cockatoo, fled into the drawing-room; two chairs were upset (one, I think, broken), Miss Sally enveloped herself in a window curtain, Philippa and Miss Shute effaced themselves beneath a table; the cockatoo, foiled of its prey, skimmed, still screeching, round the ceiling. It was Bernard who, with a well-directed sofa-cushion, drove the enemy from the room. There was only a chink of the door open, but the cockatoo turned on his side as he flew, and swung through it like a woodcock.

We slammed the door behind him, and at the same instant there came a thumping on the floor overhead, muffled, yet peremptory.

'That's Mrs Buck!' said Miss Shute, crawling from under the table; 'the room over this is the one that had the candle in it.'

We sat for a time in awful stillness, but nothing further happened, save a distant shriek overhead, that told the cockatoo had sought and found sanctuary in his owner's room. We had tea *sotto voce*, and then, one by one, despite the amazing discomfort of the drawing-room chairs, we dozed off to sleep.

It was at about five o'clock that I woke with a stiff neck and an uneasy remembrance that I had last seen Maria in the kitchen. The others, looking each of them about twenty years older than their age, slept in various attitudes of exhaustion. Bernard opened his eyes as I stole forth to look for Maria, but none of the ladies awoke. I went down to the evil-smelling passage that led to the kitchen stairs and, there on a mat, regarding me with intelligent affection, was Maria; but what—oh, what was the white thing that lay between her forepaws?

The situation was too serious to be coped with alone. I fled noiselessly back to the drawing-room and put my head in; Bernard's eyes—blessed be the light sleep of sailors!—opened again, and there was that in mine that summoned him forth. (Blessed also be the light step of sailors!)

We took the corpse from Maria, withholding perforce the language and the slaughtering that our hearts ached to bestow. For a minute or two our eyes communed.

'I'll get the kitchen shovel,' breathed Bernard, 'you open the hall door!'

A moment later we passed like spirits into the open air, and on into a little garden at the end of the house, Maria followed us, licking her lips. There were beds of nasturtiums, and of purple stocks, and of marigolds. We chose a bed of stocks, a plump bed, that looked like easy digging. The windows were all tightly shut and shuttered, and I took the cockatoo from under my coat and hid it, temporarily, behind a box border. Bernard had brought a shovel and a coal scoop. We dug like badgers. At eighteen inches we got down into shale and stones, and the coal scoop struck work.

'Never mind,' said Bernard; 'we'll plant the stocks on top of him.' It was a lovely morning, with a new-born blue sky and a light northerly breeze. As we returned to the house, we looked across the wavelets of the little cove and saw, above the rocky point round which we had groped last night, a triangular white patch moving slowly along.

'The tide's lifted her!' said Bernard, standing stock-still. He looked at Mrs Buck's window and at me. 'Yeates!' he whispered, 'let's quit!'

It was now barely six o'clock, and not a soul was stirring. We woke the ladies and convinced them of the high importance of catching the tide. Bernard left a note on the hall table for Dr Fahy, a beautiful note of leave-taking and gratitude, and apology for the broken window (for which he begged to enclose half a crown). No allusion was made to the other casualties. As we neared the strand he found an occasion to say to me:

'I put in a postscript that I thought it best to mention that I had seen the cockatoo in the garden, and hoped it would get back all right. That's quite true, you know! But look here, whatever you do, you must keep it all dark from the ladies. . . .'

At this juncture Maria overtook us with the cockatoo in her mouth.

1. The daylight is described as 'anaemic' (line 6) because
   A. it is early
   B. it is yet to come
   C. the light is pale
   D. the light is weak
   E. it depends on the candle's light

2. As 'objects of compassion' (line 8) they were in need of
   A. help
   B. advice
   C. pity
   D. money
   E. guidance

3. The point made at the end of the first paragraph is that
   A. women are superior to men
   B. the men were nervous
   C. the women were troubled by their conscience
   D. the men were held back by their conscience
   E. the men had no conscience but lacked courage

4. In the light of the rest of the passage, the use of the word 'immigrants' (line 13) is an example of
   A. exaggeration
   B. understatement
   C. sarcasm

D. humour

E. scorn

5. The 'hint of exclusiveness' (line 19) is suggested because
    A. there is a knocker and a bell
    B. the house was a rectory
    C. the house had a porch
    D. the knocker and bell do not work
    E. it was a small two-storeyed house

6. His hand is described as 'faltering' (line 22) because he is
    A. injured
    B. deformed
    C. a bad shot
    D. nervous
    E. tired

7. Miss Shute calls it a 'lunatic asylum' (line 25) because
    A. the place is isolated
    B. it has slippers on the porch
    C. the door bell and knocker do not work
    D. the response to the gravel was alarming
    E. it was a hideous building

8. The cockatoo is compared to a 'ghost' (line 31) because
    A. it is white in colour
    B. it is an unexpected sight
    C. it sat on the man's shoulder
    D. the man's appearance is odd
    E. its appearance is frightening

9. A Malay kris (line 33) is nearest in meaning to
    A. a musical instrument
    B. a sword
    C. an ornament
    D. a decorative roof-eave
    E. a tobacco pipe

10. The word 'decorously' (line 45) suggests that the visitors were
    A. attractive to look at
    B. well-dressed
    C. very attentive

91

D. on their best behaviour

E. entertained by the situation

11. The term 'unclean spirit' (line 43) has been anticipated in which of the following words in the passage?
    A. Gnome-like.
    B. Nightmare.
    C. Ushered.
    D. Misfortunes.
    E. Apparition.

12. 'Obviously remembering his costume' (line 58) refers to the implication that
    A. he was dressed in a dressing-gown
    B. he was dressed like a footman
    C. his costume was unsuitable for a doctor
    D. he had no trousers on
    E. his feet were bare

13. Mrs Buck was 'the most feared and cherished' of Dr Fahy's patients because
    A. she was wealthy
    B. she paid more than anyone else
    C. he was afraid of the cockatoo
    D. she was suffering from dementia
    E. he was very fond of her

14. 'Dr Fahy had evidently a turn for conversation that was unaffected by circumstance' (line 68) implies all the following *except*
    A. he was talkative
    B. he did not mind when he talked
    C. he often repeated himself
    D. this occasion was not suitable for conversation
    E. he talked a great deal on this occasion

15. The description of their laughter as the result of 'demonaic possession' implies that it was
    A. wicked
    B. not their own
    C. uncontrollable
    D. lunatic
    E. united

16. The implication of the sentence beginning 'There followed . . .'
(line 79) is that
  A. they all nearly fell over
  B. there was an accident
  C. their conduct was unreasonable
  D. they were weak from laughter
  E. their behaviour became irrational

17. 'A cat in some unseen fastness' (line 86) suggests that the cat was
  A. hiding
  B. in a safe place
  C. running away
  D. chasing some prey
  E. was in the dark

18. 'Noisome purlieus' (line 90) means
  A. noisy corridors
  B. heavy boots
  C. smelly clothes
  D. unpleasant places
  E. echoing cellars

19. The term 'the rookery of paying guests' (line 93) is appropriate
for all the following reasons *except*
  A. the guests are upstairs
  B. the guests are old
  C. there are a number of guests
  D. the guests all have their own rooms
  E. the guests live in a kind of community

20. The words 'malign meditation' suggests that the cockatoo was
  A. eerie
  B. single-minded
  C. sleepy
  D. prepared for trouble
  E. violent

21. The word 'peremptory' (line 117) could best be replaced by
  A. urgent
  B. clear
  C. insistent
  D. frightened
  E. unmistakable

22. The passage 'but what—oh what was the white thing that lay between her forepaws?' (line 132) is an example of
    A. anti-climax
    B. dramatic irony
    C. repetition
    D. extended metaphor
    E. rhetorical question

23. In the context of the passage, the force of the phrase 'regarding me with intelligent affection' lies in its
    A. emotional effect
    B. anticipation
    C. incongruity
    D. relevance
    E. careful observation

24. It is implied that Bernard has some of the following qualities:
    (i) He is strong.
    (ii) He is a light sleeper.
    (iii) He can move with little noise.
    (iv) He is a good sportsman.
    Is it
    A. (i) and (ii)?
    B. (iii) and (iv)?
    C. (i) and (iv)?
    D. (ii) and (iii)?
    E. (ii) and (iv)?

25. The 'slaughtering' (line 140) that they wished to bestow concerned
    A. Dr Fahy
    B. the cockatoo
    C. Mrs Buck
    D. Maria
    E. Dr Fahy's guests

26. They 'passed like spirits' (line 144) because
    A. it was night
    B. they were pale
    C. they carried a corpse
    D. they were quiet
    E. it was a strange experience

27. The passage is told
    A. in a dramatic manner
    B. in the third person
    C. in the first person
    D. by an anonymous observer
    E. in a rhetorical manner

28. In the boat party how many women are named?
    A. None.
    B. One.
    C. Two.
    D. Three.
    E. Four.

29. The note is described as 'beautiful' (line 166) because
    A. the writer is referring to the writing
    B. the wording was clever
    C. it contained an eloquent apology
    D. the writer is being sarcastic
    E. the emotions were genuinely felt

30. The humour of the passage depends mostly on
    A. character
    B. situation
    C. coincidence
    D. contrast
    E. sarcasm

Sources of Passages

1. 'The Actor' from *The Desperadoes* — Stan Barstow — Michael Joseph Ltd

2. *Gun for Sale* — Graham Greene — William Heinemann Ltd and The Bodley Head

3. *The General* — Alan Sillitoe — W. H. Allen & Co. Ltd

4. *Hurry On Down* — John Wain — Martin Secker & Warburg Ltd

5. 'The Tractor' from *Commonwealth Short Stories* — Peter Cowan — Angus Robertson (UK) Ltd and Nelson & Sons Ltd

6. *Sons and Lovers* — D. H. Lawrence — Laurence Pollinger Ltd and the Estate of the late Mrs Frieda Lawrence

7. 'Miss King' from *The Complete Short Stories of W. Somerset Maugham* — W. Somerset Maugham — The Literary Executor of W. Somerset Maugham and William Heinemann Ltd

8. *Parker Adderson, Philosopher* — Ambrose Bierce — Chatto & Windus Ltd

9. *Shakespeare of London* — Marchette Chute — © 1949 by E. P. Dutton & Co. Inc. Publishers, and used with their permission

10. *Ben Jonson and King James* — Eric Linklater — Jonathan Cape Ltd

11. *Human Groups* — W. J. H. Sprott — Penguin Books Ltd. Copyright W. J. H. Sprott, 1968

12. 'The Glory' from *Collected Poems* and 'In Time of "The Breaking of Nations"' from *Collected Poems* — Edward Thomas — Thomas Hardy — Mrs. Myfanwy Thomas and Faber & Faber Ltd — By permission of the Hardy Estate and Macmillan, London and Basingstoke

13. *Malone Dies* — Samuel Beckett — Calder and Boyars Ltd

14. *Reminiscences of an Irish R.M.* — Somerville and Ross — John Farquharson Ltd and the Estate of Somerville and Ross